Six Poetry Formats and the Transforming Image

A Monograph on Free Verse

Six Poetry Formats and the Transforming Image

A Monograph on Free Verse

Edith L. Tiempo

The University of the Philippines Press
Diliman, Quezon City

THE UNIVERSITY OF THE PHILIPPINES PRESS
E. de los Santos St., UP Campus, Diliman, Quezon City 1101
Tel. No.: 9253243 / Telefax No.: 9282558
website: www.uppress.org

The National Library of the Philippines CIP Data

Recommended entry:

Tiempo, Edith L.
Six poetry formats and the transforming image: a monograph on free verse / Edith L. Tiempo. — Quezon City: The University of the Philippines Press, c2007.
126 p.; 22.86 cm.

1. Poetics. 2. Poetry—Themes, motives. 3. Philippine poetry (English)—History and criticism. I. Title.

PN1042 808.1 2007 P065000009
ISBN 978-971-542-528-5

Book Design by Zenaida N. Ebalan

Printed in the Philippines by Econofast Press

To the memory of Robert Frost, 1874–1963

Table of Contents

Acknowledgments xi

Author's Note xv

Introduction by Vicente Garcia Groyon xvii

Six Poetry Formats and the Transforming Image 1

Format I 12

Gémino H. Abad, "Ghosts"

Rowena T. Torrevillas, "A Balloon for Rima"

Format II 26

Mark A. R. Cayanan, "Between Sleeps"

Patrizia Cavalli, "Far from kingdoms"

"Now that the time seems all mine"

Format III 34

Elizabeth Jennings, "A Game of Chess"

Robert Frost, "The Impulse"

Format IV 46

Vachel Lindsay, "The Leaden-Eyed"

Sarah Cleghorn, "The Golf Links"

Edgar Allan Poe, "The Conqueror Worm"
William Cullen Bryant, "The Murdered Traveller"

Format V 58
Ralph Waldo Emerson, "The Rhodora"
Alfred A. Yuson, "The Afternoon Gardener"
Ernesto S. Yee, "Gladiolus and Her Kind"

Format VI 68
Nick Joaquin, "The Innocence of Solomon"
Edith L. Tiempo, "Rain in Granite Country"
Francis C. Macansantos, "Fisherman's Sonnet"
Denise Levertov, "The Anteroom"

Touchstones from Contemporary Philippine Poets 85

Gémino H. Abad
Rowena T. Torrevillas
Alfred A. Yuson
Ophelia Dimalanta
Marjorie Evasco
D. M. Reyes

More Touchstones from Contemporary Philippine Poets 88

Cesar R. Aquino: "Point of View," from Checkmeta
Ernesto S. Yee, "Saprid's Man Taming the Tikbalang," last stanza, *from* Covenants

Seven Exemplary Workshop Poems 89

"She Who Jumped as a Tragedy," Jonathan Davila

"New Hampshire," George Ramos

"Iron Maiden," Ken Ishikawa

"T. S. Eliot at Lloyds," George Ramos

"Placelessness," Vincent Coscolluela

"Mother," Nicolo Vitug

"The End of a Frontier," Ken Ishikawa

To Bind the Free: By Way of Summation 97

Endnotes 100

Bibliography 103

Acknowledgments

I extend my deep gratitude and appreciation to Josephine Bendijo-Amaro and Maria Isabel Sedigo-Patelona for their thorough and painstaking efforts in encoding and otherwise preparing the manuscript of this book.

Grateful acknowledgment is hereby rendered to the following authors and publishers for the use of their excellent materials:

Alfred A. Yuson, "Afternoon Gardener," in *Sea Serpent* (Quezon City: Monsoon Press, 1980) and three "touchstone" references taken from pp. 68-69.

Cesar Aquino, "Point of View," in *Checkmeta: The Cesar Ruiz Aquino Reader* (Davao City: Midtown Printing Co., Inc., 2003), 100.

Dennis Levertov, "The Anteroom," in *Denise Levertov: Collected Earlier Poems 1940-1960* (New York: New Directions Publishing Corporation, 1979), 5-6.

Edgar Allan Poe, "The Conqueror Worm," in *A College Book of American Literature*, ed. Ellis, Pound, and Spohn, 844-45.

Edilberto K. Tiempo, Miguel Bernad, Edith Tiempo, *Introduction to Literature* (Quezon City: R.P. Garcia Publishing, 1977; Manila: Rex Bookstore, 1989).

Edith L. Tiempo, portions from "Pagsubay: Resounding Contemporary Philippine Poetic Articulating," in *Pagsubay: Graduate School Journal of the Eastern Visayas State University*, vols. 3 and 4, 2003-2004, 2004-2005, ed. David Genotiva.

Edith L. Tiempo, "Rain in Granite Country," in *Marginal Annotations* (Quezon City: Giraffe Books, 2001), 58-59.

Elizabeth Jennings, "A Game of Chess," in *Collected Poems, 1953-1985* (New York: Carcanet Press Ltd., 1987), 49-50.

Ernesto S. Yee, "Gladiolus and Her Kind," *About My Garden* (Quezon City: Giraffe Books, 2001), 26.

Ernesto S. Yee, "Saprid's Man Taming the Tikbalang," in *Covenants and Other Poems* (Quezon City: Giraffe Books, 1999), 24.

Francis A. Macansantos, "Fisherman's Sonnet," in *Father Poems*, ed. Gémino H. Abad and Alfred Yuson (Pasig City, Philippines: Anvil Publishing Inc., 2004), 57.

Gémino H. Abad, "Ghosts," *A Makeshift Sun* (Quezon City: University of the Philippines Press, 2001), 111-12.

Jacques Maritain, "*The Third Way*: By the Contingent and the Necessary," in *Approaches to God* (New York and Evanston: Harper and Row, Harper Torchbooks, 1956).

Mark A. R. Cayanan, "Between Sleeps," 2003 National Writers Workshop, Dumaguete City, Philippines.

Milton Ellis, Louise Pound, George Weida Spohn, eds., *A College Book of American Literature* (New York, Cincinnati, Chicago, Boston, Dallas, San Francisco: American Book Company, 1940).

Nick Joaquin, "The Innocence of Solomon," in *One Hundred Love Poems*, ed. Gémino H. Abad and Alfred Yuson (Diliman Quezon City: The University of the Philippines Press, 2004), 15.

Patrizia Cavalli, "Far from kingdoms" and "Now that the time seems all mine" in *The Vintage Book of Contemporary World Poetry*, ed. J.D. McClatchy (New York: Random House, Inc, 1996), 65, 67.

Ralph Waldo Emerson, "The Rhodora," in *A College Book of American Literature*, ed. Ellis, Pound, and Spohn, 632.

Robert Frost, "The Hill Wife," in Tiempo, Bernad, and Tiempo, *Introduction to Literature*, 310-12.

Robert Frost, "The Impulse," in *The Robert Frost Reader* (Library of Congress Cataloguing, Publication Data), ed. Edward Connery, 68.

Rowena T. Torrevillas, "A Balloon for Rima," in *Mountain Sacraments* (Manila: De La Salle University Press, 1991), 63-64.

Sarah Cleghorn, "The Golf Links," in Tiempo, Bernad, and Tiempo, *Introduction to Literature*, 285.

Vachel Lindsay, "The Leaden-Eyed," in Tiempo, Bernad, and Tiempo, *Introduction to Literature*, 285.

William Cullen Bryant, "The Murdered Traveller," in *A College Book of American Literature*, ed. Ellis, Pound and Spohn, 540.

Author's Note

A reader may wonder why *Six Poetry Formats and the Transforming Image* is announced as a monograph on free verse, but ends up defining the genre of poetry—that is, defining poetry as an *art form*, whatever be its purpose and benefits. It is obvious, of course, that identifying free verse as poetry requires knowing what, in the first place, is poetry itself.

The poems chosen to demonstrate the six poetry formats included here show that poetry is authenticated by its crucial two factors, without which the articulation is virtually prose. Each variant format shows what happens when the poetry piece is created without either factor (or both), or is deficient in using them.

It should be mentioned that the six formats are *consequences*—*observed* consequences—of poetry; they are not offered as handpicking "choices" to guide in writing poetry.

Whatever traditional features that free verse may choose to be free of, therefore, it follows that free verse is poetry only with the proper use of the two factors that authenticate the poetry genre.

Otherwise, in effect, with free verse as the poetic verbalizing today, it seems we are otherwise left with no inherent factors distinguishing between what is poetry and prose preening as poetry—and the nightmare apprehension that with no clear distinguishing factors the poetry genre is eventually lost altogether.

E.L.T.

Introduction*

Vicente Garcia Groyon

The deliberate poet, before writing poetry, ought to be able to answer three questions:

1. What is poetry?
2. What is good poetry?
3. How is good poetry written?

As a writer of an admittedly prosaic mindset, these questions have continued to vex me in my attempts to write, even read, poetry.

To the second and third, there are as many answers as there are poets, perhaps owing to the inclusion of the word "good." The answer to the first, though it controls those of the second and third, continues to elude many poets and critics today, even the most active and forthright. It goes without saying that the writing of poetry goes arm-in-arm with the study of poetry.

However, there is much confusion and debate over how poetry is to be taught. Often, a teacher of poetry will merely present various

---

* Mr. Groyon was a Fellow in the Dumaguete National Writers Workshop. The present monograph is chiefly intended for young writers and others who aspire to write poetry.

samples of texts currently agreed upon as poetry and point out salient features, hoping perhaps that a composite image, however hazy, may arise out of the juxtaposition. There may be vague prescriptions, or recourses to easier territory: an enumeration of figures of speech, perhaps; an identification of rhyming patterns; a discussion of theme; or an analysis of a poem's strategy and cohesiveness.

Perhaps the worst people to explain what poetry is are poets themselves, whose pronouncements are apt to be couched in idioms and laden with ambiguity and indirection. All this only intensifies the mystique of poetry, a mystique in which many aspire to cloak themselves. Certainly, when a poem succeeds at working its magic, there goes with it an inability (or reluctance) to show how the trick works. The vagueness surrounding the definition of poetry is in all probability a strategic move, for it prevents the totalizing reduction of poetry into a paint-by-numbers undertaking. Poetry, as art, tends to resist attempts at classification; the enemy of art is morphology. And yet its nature must be caught and explained if any lucid discussion is to continue. This is poetry's greatest irony—that to explain what a poem is, one must resort to prose.

The writing workshop, as transplanted to the Philippines from Iowa, has developed over the decades to become the ideal classroom for people who would learn the craft of writing. Applying the almost scientific approach of the Russian Formalists and American New Critics to the critiquing of participants' poems, workshops in the Philippines function as intensive tutorials in close reading and analysis, with the ultimate aim of improving a writer's technique.

Technique, though, because it is extremely easy to isolate, lends itself to overzealous application at the expense of other poetic principles, resulting in variants of the much-maligned "workshop poem." One such type is a poem so technically proficient that it becomes less a poem than a carefully constructed performance designed to dazzle the workshop and preempt unfavorable criticism. Another type is the poem that applies technique without understanding the nature of poetic utterance, eliciting the dreaded verdict: "This is not (yet) poetry." This verdict, it must be pointed out, returns us to the first question posed above.

The Philippines in recent years has seen a steady rise in the number of young people who would write poetry, especially free verse, even as the number of poetry readers dwindles. As with any new generation, there are gestures of resistance to "older," "established" forms and styles (usually as represented by Formalism and New Criticism), efforts to break through to a poetry of and about the strange times in which the poet lives. But despite the turn toward a new Romanticism eager to experiment and release poetry from the clutches of technique, answering the questions posed above demands an inexorable return to the very nature of poetry and the poetic.

It is this inevitable doubling back and starting over that the present monograph hopes to facilitate. Here, as in no other study of poetry, the patient reader will find the primary question answered with clarity, authority, and good humor.

A detailed explication, particularly one that classifies, risks mummifying the art. However, *Six Poetry Formats and the Transforming*

Image demonstrates that to dissect poetry and lay bare its elements is not necessarily to kill it. While science has named just about every part of the human body, certain elusive components remain beyond its grasp. In this comprehensive catalogue, Dr. Edith L. Tiempo cages the poetic but allows its animating spark, its soul, to fly free. Thus liberated, the poem might attain the heights it aspires to, while remaining firmly, undeniably poetry.

Manila
9 March 2006

Six Poetry Formats and the Transforming Image

In the forty-five years of its existence the National Writers Workshop has been intermittently asked, at least once during the three-week sessions, to answer a certain question: "How can we tell if it is really poetry?" And each time, the question is bestowed the same answer defining just the basic character of poetry as we see this genre today, and for the moment bypassing its more critical demands on subtlety, indirection, fresh insights, and the special use of other literary instruments like thematic tension, understatement, ambiguity, tone control, among many other intricate sophistications; these finer-spun minutiae are explained and understood in a more spontaneous and natural way in the course of the discussions on the submitted poems. So far, this answering procedure seems to satisfy.

The questions being asked about distinguishing the literary genres are recurrent concerns in writing courses and workshops and are more often raised in regard to poetry, since fiction, long and short, is unmistakably prose. Poetry is a different matter because its articulation tends to *apparently* straddle prose as well (i. e., in free verse), so that it is indeed difficult at times to tell when the piece is actually prose preening as poetry. As a matter of fact, there are those, especially among our talented younger writers, turning out some really impressive pieces, who write their poems unaware of generic consequence, blissfully unknowing when they are actually writing prose. For in any creative work, sticking to the genre is of course requisite because the genre is a category of *art*. For one, the literary genre distinguishes its artistic varieties from each other, i. e., *poetry* and fictional and expository *prose*. Obviously, therefore, the poetic piece that is not shaped according to the terms of the poetry genre, *no matter how impressively worded*, cannot result in art but in a kind of prose-articulating that could be classifiable (*horrors!*) with TV yak gazettes and glossy stereotypical trade news sheets, and pontifical academic and church bulletins, and slogging ROTC manuals.

Likewise, the fictional writing follows the demands of the genre of fiction; otherwise, the result is—alack—not poetry, but just bad fiction writing.

At this point, I must beg pardon for bringing up familiar and elementary facts in defining the mechanical earmarks of poetry. The information provides the necessary background for considering the six poetry formats presented here.

By way of a mark-off, the literary form we speak of today as poetry—as distinguished from the epic and the dramatic—is considered a development from what was designated as lyric poetry, with its strongly formative musical elements, and was originally meant to be sung. Today's poetry still involves distinctly music-related attributes such as rhythm, metrical beat, rhyme, euphony, alliteration, onomatopoeia, repetition, assonance, dissonance, and other functional sound effects.

The question being raised today about poetry and what is poetic, and the answer to it, have been so repeatedly reconnoitered that we wonder how the subject could continue hatching problems of related significance, or rehashing them, like the present concern on the governance of literary genres—specifically, the genre of poetry as distinguished from prose. For, in the practice of free verse, the loosening of certain traditional bounds provokes naturally enough the apprehensive thought that—the Muse forbid!—poetry, despite being distinguished by its intricate phrasings and sophisticated insights, is insidiously losing its territory to prose, that it could be confronting obliteration as a distinct art genre and end up as a new and precious form of prose, poetry-sounding but nonetheless prose. Not at all a far-fetched possibility except for the judicious craftsmanship of the poets among us who keep the bogey at bay with their works of undisputed free-verse poetry, the bulk of which includes *prose-sounding* poetry.

To be sure, there has never existed a sacrosanct poetic form; starting from even before poetry was first recorded—Chinese, Japanese, Greek, Sufi, occasionally, the Indian sloka, the Indonesian pantun, etc.—these poetic works have never followed one identifiable, specified mandated form, none except of their own respective making. So what common ingredient identifies them as poetry and not prose? And we are not thinking about verse-line format as the distinguishing feature, since prose has also been cut up into so-called poetry lines by unknowing practitioners.

Much of the material brought up in these introductory pages may sound like rather banal repetitions, but are relevant in considering the six poetry formats presented here.

We know that Aristotle has differentiated the two genres by their respective substance and function, designating one as poetry and the other as history. Today, our idea of poetry subsumes history—and prose fiction is also still a distinct genre.

Whatever the substance and format, what is therefore the fundamental element that does make poetry the unique species of literary art that it is? Fortunately, as we see it today, the question is quickly answerable regarding the bottom agent responsible and, as they say, No sweat: Prose is direct statement and direct exposition, *whether written in versified lines* or in paragraphs. On the other hand, poetry has traditionally been acknowledged as indirect, as structured in metaphor; that is, the crucial idea of the poem—be it presented as plain statements—is articulated in metaphor, and that makes all the difference. A close scrutiny and research into our contemporary poetry and the poetry of the recent past show that in the poetic procedure, metaphor, manifested as *image* (or picture or situation), transforms the prosaic into poetic. The simplest definition, then, seems to be: Poetic versifying is casting the material in metaphor—or in image, if you will; dramatic, suggestive image or situation that transforms the prose into poetry. Thus we go by the fundamental distinction today, as authenticated in the creative procedures of our contemporary poetry and of the poetry of the recent past.

Without the structuring of metaphor there is no poetry.

The question is asked: In the first place, why has poetry bypassed the direct pronouncement of prose statements and chosen the indirect portraying of metaphor? The major reason of course is obvious—**metaphor enhances.** It goes beyond the bare presentation of literal statement and allows and facilitates the reader's right to make his own creative response, thereby in a real sense lending individual enhancement to the metaphor, and the created work itself.

The very simplified material following below is not meant to "talk down"; again, it is relevant to the constituency of the six poetry formats.

About metaphorical structuring, how does it work? How does it develop the poetic meaning? As explained earlier, and as may be gathered from the various listed formats described and demonstrated below, the metaphoric procedure operates in the way of all metaphors: one, through image or situation that is charged with symbolic meaning; two, in its own singularly heightened way it uses "internal" literary instruments to develop the poem's meaning. More on these "internal" instruments later.

Unbelievable as it seems, there was a very capable young writer who still asked to be shown how the metaphor works in a poem; or, he was, most commendably, just being conscientious about "seeing" the largely invisible ramifications of the shift from statement to metaphor. "How does the image or situation turn into a metaphor?" was asked in heart-tugging (mostly feigned) befuddlement. Scrabbling for the simplest example, I dredged up from among two or three other choices Longfellow's "The Arrow and the Song":

The Arrow and the Song

I SHOT an arrow into the air,
It fell to earth, I knew not where;
For, so swiftly it flew, the sight
Could not follow it in its flight.

I breathed a song into the air,
It fell to earth, I knew not where;
For who has sight so keen and strong,
That it can follow the flight of song?

Long, long afterward, in an oak
I found the arrow, still unbroke;
And the song, from beginning to end,
I found again in the heart of a friend.

"Now," I asked the budding poet, "is this prose?—that is, is it telling a factual, literal account?"

"Of course not." He quoted: " 'And the song, from beginning to end,/I found again in the heart of a friend'—How could that be a literal factual statement, even with the help of a cardiology surgeon?"

"Then what is it saying?"

"That's blatantly obvious: One's acts, I suppose especially good acts, tend to persist, they are not lost."

"You have just transformed the poem's image and situation into the metaphoric framework."

"What do you mean? I didn't see it happen."

"Of course you did. Because we know *arrow* is not literal arrow, nor is *song* literal. The image and situation in each stanza are your metaphors to reveal the poem's **meaningful assertion**, to assert its **focus of meaning**, its **concept**—which you just verbalized."

"Ah-!" And he repeats, "... for the poem's meaning ... Gotcha, I suppose."

"And we all know that not all good poems are as simple. But basically that's your 'metaphoring'."

"I—I suppose—I mean, yes, *of course*. And *directly stating or recounting the meaningful assertion in factual, literal statements*, though written in verse lines, makes it prose."

"You may now pull out the nail you've hit on the head. For the next time if needed, you know."

Concerning the generic tension between poetry and prose, and with apologies to the mentors and practitioners who have already batted around-and-about this recurrent issue, particularly as it arises in free verse, this article suggests a simplified way to distinguish between the poetry-like *prose* and the prose-like *poetry*. (And in the face of the rampant use of literal statements we are not considering the mechanical verse-lines format as necessarily a valid distinguishing feature.) Presented here are poems that demonstrate what *seems* like territorial encroachment and what *is* actual encroachment.

More apologies: I did not invent the various mechanical formats of poetry that are presented here; these six listed formats are not hypothetical but have been gathered from the existent practices of contemporary poems and of poems of the recent past.

The concern here is not with the standardized formats like the villanelle, the sonnet, the sestina, and other forms that have long been mechanically set and stabilized. Our interest is in the formats that allow for flexibility in their formatting, the reason for this being apparent.

But first of all, a bit of explication about what is listed here as *poetic formats*. Their character and significance are best understood after first taking a look at the poetic operation itself. More apologies at this point for the necessity to lay bare the guts, the intestines of poetry itself.

Two concerns are involved in the forming of the poem: One, any of the various kinds of formats presented here (or any other that the poem may take). The list that follows presents the formats merely as mechanical descriptions.

Two, the more crucial aspect of the poetic operation has to do with revealing the concept or the poem's meaning. And traditionally acknowledged as instrumental in materializing this concept is the functioning of heightened language and heightened sensibility; these attributes are observed to be effected in the use of the "internal" artistic instruments already mentioned, like thematic tension, understatement, ambiguity, indirection, and tone control, among others. So it is the concept's necessities that dictate the particular use of these critical tools; thus, the conceptual aspect and the mechanical format are the two basic involvements.

These two basic involvements are simply demonstrated by taking a quick look at the poem, at the structure of its format, and at its concept, *poem* being briefly envisioned in the abstract at this point. Inherent in the nature of the poetic structure are two consistent earmarks which are best designated here as the "external" and the "internal" limits. The external earmarks involve the particular mechanical format being used, which covers the length and formation of the lines (minimalist lines or long lines, stanzas or interludes), and of course the conventional features of meter, rhyme, rhythm, and, for special use, euphonic diction patterns (Poe's "... bells, bells, bells ..."), as well as juxtaposition, and typographical idiosyncracies. These are the *external* limits, the earmarks that are more visible on the page.

The *internal* limits serve the conceptual aspect and have to do with the use of the less "visible" elements already mentioned, like tone, nuances, understatement, suggestiveness, indirection, thematic tension, contrast, ellipses, fresh stratagems and insights, inventive reproductive use of words, among many other subtleties and effects that shape the poetic meaning of the piece. For the purpose of analysis we have separated the two limits here, but in the act of creating, they obviously work synchronously.

The poems being used here for demonstrating the six formats are selected not necessarily because the authors are noted writers—even if they happen to be—but only because the poems are clear examples, respectively, of the formats being demonstrated.

The following list provides the description of the individual features of the six formats and their respective results. As mentioned, the list is formulated from the practices manifested in existing representative contemporary poems and in poems of the recent past. (Expanded discussions on the critical features of the instantiating poems augment the purely mechanical description of the six listed formats.)

Description of the six formats noted in late recorded poetry

I. Without the use of the conventional external limits of rhyme, meter, and other traditional features like regular stanza pattern, special imagery and diction, the internal limits and the metaphorical framework take over. Result: poetry in free verse.

II. Also in free verse: with or without using internal limits—and without the metaphoric structure. Result: prose.

III. With rhymed and metered lines regularized; with internal limits; with metaphoric structure. Result: poetry well crafted.

IV. Also using rhymed, metered lines; with or without internal limits—and without the metaphoric structure. Result: prose

V. With rhymed and metered lines; with metaphoric structure; with inadequate or no purposeful use of internal limits. Result: poetry of neat but rather uninventive craftsmanship.

VI. A species of free verse: in metaphoric structure; with rhymed lines or other traditional features; with or without meter; with internal limits; the lines expressed as prose-like statements. Result: poetry well crafted.

Notes on the six poetry formats described above

- No. I is good free verse, the procedure used by practically all our fine poetry being written today.
- No. II is the kind of "free-verse poetry" being written mostly by those of our very promising young writers when unaware that they are virtually writing prose—and "bad

prose" as it turns out, or so would protest some scandalized die-hard fictionists who would have their fictional prose articulated by unversified plain straightforward statements in *paragraph* format.

- No. III is the procedure followed by well-written traditional poetry.
- No. IV is the pickle that traditionally disposed poetry gets into without the transforming metaphoric frame.
- No. V is structurally good uncluttered writing, but in missing out on a more inventive use of the internal poetic instruments, it creates poetry that easily "could-have-been-great."
- No. VI is a variant procedure of free verse in which this writer, for one, currently finds room for both *discipline* (using rhymed lines or other traditional features) and *spontaneity* (mostly using lines expressed in prose-like statements)—and finds the result intellectually and emotionally suitable.

Result: a species of free verse using rhyme or other traditional features as a controlling safeguard from "carefree-versing" into prose.

A quick scrutiny of the list shows that the formats that result in prose lack, or are deficient in, one or both of the two poetry indicators that authenticate the other poetry formats: metaphorical structuring, and heightened language and heightened sensibility generated in the use of "internal" literary instruments. Both precepts are found to be integral in the format types that result in poetry.

The six designs presented here could serve as a kind of short-cut reference to show if a poem (especially when written in free verse) is an encroachment of prose into poetry territory. All this helps in keeping a weather-eye on poetry as a distinctly defined genre of art.

Exemplifying the Formats, Numbers I to VI.

Format I. Free verse, the current poetry format.

Format Ia. "Ghosts," Gémino H. Abad

Ghosts

I always see them
at the corner of my eyes,
so sudden, so far
I hardly catch a glimpse
—but human still,
flitting past ...
gossamer of guilt?
tatterdemalion of days?

I must needs go back
to my poet's occupation
and forget.

But ah, yes,
what visitants did I see?
scrimmage of gutter kids
in traffic snarls?
chiaroscuro of mourners
at a deserted wake?

What trick of eye, or ear,
or random stab of memory?
Through the bright hurt
of summer on shanties
along a disused railway—
the drift and fall
of too human dust?

No, only sun's filigree
visible in a slant of light,
quickly gone.
If wisps of their shape
still shape a something human,
my words must crave more
than sparkle and glint
at their azury offing,
or there isn't any accounting
for our sun's drizzle of dust.
      No gossamer
where words cannot web.

—From A *Makeshift Sun*

In the poem the "ghosts" that haunt the poet-persona are certain scenes and details and sensations that come to mind as they break into his creative labors and try to usurp his "poet's occupation." The persona makes an initial effort to forget the "ghosts" but is beset instead by speculations about these shadowy "visitants"; these are ghostly, not just because they are, manifestly, mere recollections and speculations, and moreover, of things mostly "dead and gone," but more pointedly, because they are not "visible"; likewise, they are ghosts in the sense that, unbidden visitants as they are, they come conspicuously imbued with a touch of the apocalyptic, they are consistent with imminent or actual termination, with decay, with the aftermath, the "drift and fall/of too human dust."

The poem is speaking of the persistence of the past and of certain creative, if conditional encroachments on the present, although saying it suggestively, with masterly indirection through the central symbolically meaningful situation and the gravid images.

The whole situation is placed in metaphoric structure that pictorially proves rather than states the designed meaning of the poem: Structured metaphorically, *the* theme or focus of meaning is actually a proclaimed ars poetica. In a very viable sense, *the meaning of the poem, "Ghosts,"* ***posits an ars poetica asserting the influence of past and present sensibilities, and only under particular critical conditions*** *can they shape the mood and texture—if not the substance itself—of veritable insights still in the process of creation.*

The discussion that follows shows this *meaning* (bodied as the proclaimed ars poetica) as it is developed within its metaphoric frame.

Besides its metaphorical structure, the poem is also replete with crucial details heightened and enhanced, and shaped and textured, by "internal" poetic tools in the intricate course of materializing the theme and the whole poetic experience. A look at the more revelatory of these details which are "textured" by five of the poetic instruments:

1. **The preponderance of words** that address here both the physical and metaphysical decrepitude and run-down condition and frangibility of the ("ghostly") intrusive images and sensations.

    "flitting past/gossamer of guilt"
    "tatterdemalion of days"

"scrimmage of gutter kids/in traffic snarls"
 [in immediate danger of death by accident]
"chiaroscuro of mourners/at a deserted wake"
"random stab of memory"
"... shanties/along a disused railway"

2. **Juxtaposition and contrast**, in introducing "light" (for visualizing the human shape) into the dominant presence of "darkness" (the unsubstantial ghosts).

"the bright hurt/of summer on shanties"
"sun's filigree/visible in a slant of light"
"sparkle and glint"

3. The brightness and clarity of the details in no. 2, sprinkled as it were into the dark ambience of ghosts, precipitate the emergence of the **thematic tension.**

4. **Ambivalence and ambiguity**:

In the first stanza, the word "gossamer" (*of guilt*) is a "dark" term, functioning as related to ghosts and tenuousness.

But in the last stanza, "gossamer" is definitely turned ambiguous by its reverberating link to both "light" and "dark."

5. The unobtrusive presence of **internal rhyme and alliteration** wherever the lines are specially cogent.

"tatter**d**emalion of **d**ays"
"of **s**ummer on **s**hanties"
"the **d**rift and fall/of too human **d**ust"
"vi**s**ible in a **s**lant of light"
"If wi**sps** of their **s**ha**p**e"
"... our sun's **d**rizzle of **d**ust"
"**W**here **w**ords cannot **w**eb"

Parenthetically, this poem confirms that poets well into the craft no longer *consciously* employ the "internal" poetic instruments. The most effective use of these artistic tools betokens assimilation; their functioning is an intrinsic act of the creator, as is plainly so in the making of "Ghosts."

There is more to see. These are only five of a number of poetic instruments inventive in this author's word-manipulating. A scrutiny of even just the five affirms the metaphoric structure and "internal" poetic tools as the two major agents that designed "Ghosts" as distinctive and authoritative free-verse poetry—as indeed the judicious operation of these two features prove to be the crucial and major aspects that verify all good poetry.

The final portion of the job of creating the poem focuses on the intricate vehicle that embodies the theme, i. e., the gratuities of the posited ars poetica. At this point, the thematic tension is fully defined, thus: ghosts (meaning the intrusive sensibilities), even sun-gilded ghosts, are mere whisper-simulations and cannot credibly express the lineaments of the human shape: Only certain words of the artist can do that, words powerful to create or recreate the compelling visibility of these ghosts—*but only if these muscular words of the artist perform better than the "sparkle and glint"* which are derivatives from the original source of light, the sun in its "azury offing." And this ars poetica proclaims that, thus enflamed, the words superseding sparkle and glint so create the human shape. The ars poetica intimates that the crucial point of the process is this: Only the words that venture beyond all other inspirited words can account for *our* sun's being inherently besmirched by "ghostliness" (the "*drizzle of dust*").

So further: Why suddenly the resplendent sun's besmirched ("ghostly") attribute? The answer affirms the operation of two other "internal" instruments, *paradox* and *inversion*, thus: What is specified is *our* sun, not *the* sun, for the latter is the source of light and clarity and is never ghostly. On the other hand, *our* sun, which is implicitly claimed by the poet-persona on behalf of his word-weaving ilk, is characteristically perceived as bespattered with the dregs and drizzling dust of the creative process. Moreover, this posited ars poetica declares that such smears and obscurities are necessary and natural for *our* sun in igniting the blaze beyond luminosity, beyond "sparkle and glint."

And still further, one more turn in fashioning the poem's final revelation:

> *No gossamer*
> *where words cannot web.*

Together with the word, "web," the ambiguous "gossamer" prepares for the ambiguous turn that delivers this poem's ultimate meaning—an assertion that, in an intriguing sense, underlies all poetic creating. This is to say that the sly word, "web," in all its ambivalent meanings, affirms here the primal linguistic paradox—because words indeed do web, although—alack! and praise be!—not the touchable palpable shape, but webbing, only and evermore, a just and kindly deception—a "gossamer," yet a touch beyond and above truth.

This is a terrific poem, its concept relatedly evokes other facets, and the whole poetic experience is profound and intricate and withal articulated in the rich and most economical method—metaphorically, through packed images, and the operation of poetry's "internal instruments."

Sparely built and compact, the short sharp lines deliver their innocent-sounding but explosive load of artistic/human truth and linguistic ambiguity.

Clearly the free-verse structure here is exemplary in its use of the two traditional qualities found to be basic in the poetry genre.

Format Ib. "A Balloon for Rima," Rowena T. Torrevillas

Of course, the format of any poem-in-the-making is a crucial matter. And it is absurd to think a suitable format is achieved conveniently by the poet's feckless act of choosing the likely one out of a list of six formats, or even by formulating or prefabricating one. Rather, the format design comes as the poet's own immanent modus preferment, practically an instinctive decision shaping the poem's creative directions as the development moves under the requirements of the poetry genre. The format is a ***consequence***, it is not "adopted" nor a handpicking "choice."

A Balloon for Rima

Heart's wonder tugging
At a thin string's end,
Small fist curled round
Its first precarious try
At language: ***Balloon***, you cry,

Balloon! Call up the word,
Sound's careless arcane magic,
Enclosing worlds
Inside its colored skin,

Of flight held in
And running moon,
And sun swimming high
In its morning bath
Of joy, and all the earth
Bluegreen with newness—

Small hand, hold fast
To what is good,
Your speechless cry
Of pain or want:

This membrane, speech,
It breaks too soon;
A small red world
Has done its worst
Past all undoing
And rueful recall:

One new balloon is all
It takes,
To free or burst
The bright, betraying splendor
Of the Word.

The theme of "A Balloon for Rima" centers on the nature of language; the whole poem is a dramatic insight into the *word* and its attributes and its almost mystical involvement in the conduct of human life as inherent in our daily use of speech.

The child and her balloon are the central details in the poem's metaphorical structuring of this concept. As in the poem, "Ghosts," that evokes crucial perceptions about linguistic equivocalness, "A Balloon for Rima" also discloses the ambivalent nature of language and the significance of this inconsistency for man, its user.

How does the structuring in metaphor operate here in developing the poem's ultimate revelation? Obviously, the portrayal of the child's first attempt at naming the object "balloon," and manipulating it, renders the symbolical situation of man defining his relationship to the *word*, thus: the "balloon," representing the word, is symbolically perceived as the magical repository of all that mankind's sensibilities could continually discover and own of the world of nature and of life's circumstances, and above all, of the arresting facets of meaningfulness—sometimes contending and mutually opposed—that inspirit these circumstances: "Enclosing worlds/Inside its colored skin"; and in counterpart, "... hold fast/To what is good,/Your *speechless* cry/of pain and want" (italics mine).

In fact, the child's "first precarious try/At language: '**Balloon**,' you cry,/'**Balloon** ...'" recalls many an anxious writer's concern over the precarious fate of a "trial balloon" that he has attempted writing. Indeed, the child's balloon as symbol is variously appropriate for the abundant meanings it yields—startling and profound and hard-nosed meanings evoked here by such a tenuous and perishable object.

The crucial poetic instrument at work in developing the poem's concept, and the related meanings it resonates, is the instrument of *inversion*, which is the mainstay of the metaphorical functioning. The concept is gradually developed in the specific recounting of the attributes of the *word* (these various qualities made explicit in analogy with the attributes of the balloon); the tool of inversion duly turns these attributes as simultaneously both positive and ambivalent in character, and presents them in the form of concrete objects and sensations, in this way relating them to the human experiencing.

The concept's metaphorical structuring is clearly understood when we see the inversion at work, as in the following details eliciting the pleasurable, and then the "doubtful," responses in the same framework:

Purely pleasurable

1. "arcane magic," which the *word* acquires whenever (as represented by the balloon) it is "called up" to proclaim the natural world's breathtaking beauty and joy
2. "Inside its colored skin"
3. The renewal of perception:
    - "In its morning bath/Of joy ..."
    - "... and all the earth/Bluegreen with newness"

Ambivalent/conditional

1. The word/balloon's fugacious and transient nature:
    - "flight held in"
    - "running moon"
    - "sun swimming high"
    - "this membrane, speech,/It breaks too soon"
    - "Past all undoing/And rueful recall:"
    - "To free or burst/The bright, betraying splendor/Of the Word"

2. The balloon's round shape is a paradoxical wholeness entirely dependent upon the substance of air, and upon at-oneness with the outer air that is the balloon's context.

3. The "membrane-skin" of the balloon can collapse at any moment and reduce the wholeness to smithereens "past all undoing/And rueful recall."

4. The *colorful skin*: the balloon's promise of bright offerings is only *skin*-deep, and the attractive *color* recalls perceptions that are dubious and suspect, like "colored opinions" and "judgments colored" and "reactions colored" by personal animus.

5. Ironically, the balloon is free to float in air, only because of its "flight held in"; its very free-wheeling is secured by the restraining *strings attached*, which is the literal and figurative conditionality that paradoxically guarantees its freedom as it flies in space.

In connection with child and balloon, the two items dramatizing the thematic situation, the question may be asked on the considered choice of a child to enact this productive experience of discovery. Why not a grown person with an exploring mind such as the poet-persona in "Ghosts"? The justification for any choice is seen in the mutating complexion of certain words as they are created into the substance and spirit of poetry—or rather, as various practitioners and critics individually perceive their operation in poetry. To show why the choice of the child, the critic's pronouncement that is most relevant to our particular poem comes from Robert Frost, who declares that writing a poem is a game of chance, a gamble with words. Moreover, in another context, we find his lines, "And the work is play for mortal stakes," and I would like to believe that his term, "work," does include poetry and, indeed, that poetry is also "play," the activity most natural in the life of a child, a game, as with the child in this poem manipulating the chancy object, "balloon," flying in space and naming it.

Further, writing poetry is a kind of autarchic game or gamble with features that are significant in literary practice: As we know, in the interest of poetic wholeness and unity, certain words in the poem—the key words—function judiciously toward developing the central experience of the poem (its theme or meaning). But more often than is foreseen, an intriguing process ensues; by entirely fortuitous happenstance, these key words, and even words in minor positions, often independently generate relationships with one or another word or words, and they meaningfully interlock, producing other ideas and connotations that do often contribute to an even more viable wholeness and unity. (To be sure, these unbidden elements may also hamstring certain strategies in the poem!)

Moreover, words, *en solus,* sometimes interlock with other words and ideas *outside* of the poem's framework, evoking new slants that enhance the thematic intention. Below are examples of these "venturesome" words preempting, centripetally as it were, related "outside" ideas that readers may just catch "on the fly":

1. "balloon" and "precarious try," taken together, generate the very relevant idea about some anxious writer's experimental work, literally known as "trial balloon."

2. "balloon" recalls the purported words of a character in a comics strip; the words are enclosed in a circle called a "balloon" in printer's parlance.
3. "string's end" calls up the conditional "strings attached" to an otherwise decisive judgment or resolution. A related example follows below, where "strings" and "colored skin" also evoke this conditionality.
4. "colored skin" slides quite easily into "skin-deep" and (as mentioned in no. 3 of the ambivalent/conditional list above) into the "colored" or equivocal or aberrant tendencies of even scrupulously considered observations.

And so, in the light of these "chancy" attributes of the word, the choice of a child for a central image in this poem may be understood—and confirmed by an authoritative critic's view of creative writing as in itself a kind of playful risking.

Finally, the instrument of inversion performs its crucial feat which has to do with the attitude of the poem turned around to settle its final posture: *From asserting speech and sound it shifts to asserting speechlessness. From the stirring images of nature proclaimed by the wondrous words of speech, the poem shifts to disavowal of speech and affirms instead the natural and reliable truth-telling of "speechlessness,"* thus:

> Small hand, hold fast
> To what is good,
> Your *speechless* cry
> Of pain and want:

This membrane, speech,
It breaks too soon ... (italics mine)

In "... hold fast/To what is good," the "good" is indicated as the "speechless" motivation behind the unspoken word, and that motivation ("pain," "want") is real and good in itself, whereas if spoken, the word used to express this "good" may not hold good, it could be misconstrued by the hearer. So hold fast to the motivations behind the words, they are real and genuine, where the words in themselves may not hold true.

The final disavowal wrought by the tool of inversion declares the ever-present catastrophic conditionality of human speech which, like the balloon, is inherently subject to imminent destruction:

One new balloon is all
It takes,
To free or burst
The bright, betraying splendor
Of the Word.

By this fearless and rather fractious summation, the poem, through its diverse insights and paradoxical illuminations, proclaims the word's ultimate splendor and value (to *free* or *burst,* sublimated by the initial capital in Word)—word splendid and valuable, not despite but *because* of its intrinsic proximity to decay. Its fitful and changeable nature leaves the speaker, the writer—if he be rewarded—to cautiously enjoy maintaining consistent respect and care and meticulousness in its use.

Format II. This format describes the kind of "free-verse poetry" that results when the writers are unaware that they are actually writing prose. Included here is a fine example of well-crafted free verse.

Format IIa. "Between Sleeps," Mark A. R. Cayanan

Format II virtually encapsulates the problem that is the concern of this monograph, for it cites certain irresolute practices and mostly imperceptible little heresies usually committed in writing free verse. Two of the three poems that follow below demonstrate respectively the specific ways their structures went improper, and likewise, how they are inadequate in the use of the two basic qualities that have marked the genre, as manifested in recorded poetry. Of the three poems, one is excellent free verse. As already mentioned, the two primary indicators are: heightened language and sensibility, which are consequent on the poet's spontaneous manipulation of "internal" poetry instruments, and a properly structured metaphorical framework.

The author of "Between Sleeps" is a talented young poet. Portions of his beginning work display refreshing insights, and clearly show a natural turn for intricate discerning; by the same token, the craftsmanship shows the need for certain pointed directions.

Between Sleeps

Turning to bed late one night, I find you
sleeping. As lightly as my tired
body allows it, I tug at the pillow you hold
close to your chest and crawl into
the space I have created for myself.

With a few stray strands of light uncoiled
from a bulb I've kept on, I can see
the contours of your face shadowed
by repose, stilled into position:
your mouth seems to have forgotten
what is about to be said, I incline
my head towards yours to chance upon
this secret speech. The low humming
from your throat, the occasional
moans divorced from silence by small
degrees, even the almost-sour breath:
they tell me how deep into dream you are.

By now, you might be in some place where color
has the full-bodied figure it wishes
to assume, where even the most peripheral
images slide into a center surrounding you,
crowding you even. I allow myself entry,

your inner spoon, and I know where I am:
I form the umbra of this mirror
image of a question mark; I am a shape
that, with you, mars the weave,
the gray of the bedspread. Where your mind
moves, however, I can only guess.

I can opt for hope, and give my dream
of your dream a countenance: mine.
Or I can admit that somewhere between
And inside you, there are phantoms:
present and future desires and dread,
whose vivid presences are unmasked only to you,
and are then gone.

Love, I shall fall into my own
sleep knowing of you only: your inert
body leaning, relaxing onto mine.
Your hand on my belly.
Chest against back.
Shoulder towards shoulder.
Your breath and my nape.

First of all, stanzas 1 to 3 are very plainly prose articulations cut up into a versified-line format that is not regulated by the contingencies of verse-cutting—like, where does one begin and end a line, with which word does a line end, and which word introduces the next line? Naturally, not every single line has to be so crafted; nevertheless, certain lines and phrases are expected to be so crafted, those that notably carry the burden of substance in developing the poem's focus of meaning.

Second, the stanzas are clearly unmetaphored and, since no heightened articulations enhance the three stanzas, they function in the context as veritable prose in stanza form. As previously mentioned, a poem's meaningfully enhanced language and insights are consequent on the poet's spontaneous use of the "internal" poetry instruments; the three stanzas lack the directed language and inventiveness characteristic of these vital instruments at work.

But the fourth stanza shows an immediate shift toward the poetic strategy. The initial lines suddenly prove the creative hand of the poet, unmistakably recognized in the way the words and phrases move with the authoritative manipulation that sets apart the poetic utterance:

> ... I allow myself entry,
>
> your inner spoon, and I know where I am:
> I form the umbra of this mirror
> image of a question mark; I am a shape
> that, with you, mars the weave,
> the gray of the bedspread. Where your mind
> moves, however, I can only guess.

The stanza is replete with meaningful expressions like "your inner spoon," "I form the umbra of this mirror/image of a question mark," phrases that metaphorically depict the way the persona snuggles against the sleeping partner, his own body curved in accommodating itself to the relaxed contour of the sleeper. Even more:

Why "spoon" and why "question mark"? Beyond these two words' depiction of the two bodies' contoured quietness, and specifying "*inner* spoon," is the seeking to scoop into the sleeper's sanctum of dreams; and of course "question mark" is the persona's questing for revelations from that inaccessible retreat.

Juxtaposing this stanza with the initial three stanzas reveals plainly the prosiness of the preceding portions. The difference is that this fourth stanza has put the inventive poetic tools and the metaphoring operation to work.

Somehow the last stanza, which is couched mostly in declarative statements, blends into the poetic environment established in the fourth stanza. Eloquently, these final straightforward rounding-out statements deliver the poem's rendered meaning, which is (despite "I allow myself entry"): *The ultimate unknowability of the human geist remains inviolate; though the body be intimately known, the core of being is ever mysterious and impenetrable.*

Definitely a promising piece, and excellent for our purpose of demonstration.

Format IIb. "Far from kingdoms" and "Now that the time seems all mine," Patrizia Cavalli

So far we have been presented with three poems in free verse, all exemplary, with the third one, "Between Sleeps," showing portions that lapse into prose statements resulting from the inconsistent use of the "internal" instruments of poetry.

The following are two poems also in free verse, written by the renowned Italian poet Patrizia Cavalli. The first is an arresting poem of seven well-crafted lines, "Far from kingdoms." The poem is about "discover(ing) the sweetness/of many imperfections." It is amazing how the poem has packed into the brief seven lines so much dynamic evocations, all thematically significant nuances; and largely responsible are the internal poetry tools of *inversion* and *contrast*, the latter mostly subtle and implied. It is not surprising that inversion and contrast are the operational instruments, since the theme itself is an inversion.

Far from kingdoms

Far from kingdoms
how steady is the room!
Come, breathe close with me
so I may discover the sweetness
of many imperfections, some missing
tooth, some extra wrinkle, and your body
worn out slightly by carelessness.

The very first two lines signal the paradoxical theme by delineating the contrast between perfection and imperfection and the preference for the latter, thus: "kingdoms" represents perfection and "room" represents imperfection; and very deftly, the second line signals the ultimate affirmation of things imperfect by describing the (imperfect) symbolical "room" with the adjective "steady." Of course at this initial stage, all this is still mostly anticipated and subliminal for the reader.

The adjuration, "Come," in the third line suggests at least two things: first, that the discovery of the sweetness of imperfection is not possible if not actually confronted by imperfection itself. Thus, and secondly: for the discovery to be personally experienced, the word "Come" materializes the idea of imperfection in the summons for an actual person to "breathe close" with the persona in the intensity of the discovering.

The internal instrument of inversion is overall at work in affirming the imperfect as a "sweet" experience—*tooth missing, extra wrinkle*, and the coup de grace, "*your body/worn out slightly by carelessness.*"

The last imperfect item is specially rich in its thematic implications. For one, it asserts the fact that the body in its imperfect state is not devoid of perfection, but is merely "worn out *slightly*," and worn out not by inherent deficiency but by "carelessness." Further, the word "carelessness" may also imply, in a rather intriguing sense, that the condition of imperfection cares for no preservative upkeep (or "non-keep") to retain its sweetness. Of course, being preferred choices, these imperfect details are all of them inverted sensibilities that startle but are nonetheless genuinely indicative of the persona's unique discrimination and perception.

The poem is a demonstration of free verse at its best—showing the functioning of its neat metaphorical structure and of the internal artistic tools, the two thorough and crucial instruments in shaping this masterly piece.

Now that the time seems all mine

Now that the time seems all mine
and no one calls me for lunch or dinner,
now that I can stay to watch
how a cloud loosens and loses its color,
how a cat walks on the roof
in the immense luxury of a prowl, now
that what waits for me every day
is the unlimited length of a night
where there is no call and no longer a reason
to undress in a hurry to rest inside
the blinding sweetness of a body that waits for me,

now that the morning no longer has a beginning
and silently leaves me to my plans,
to all the cadences of my voice, now
suddenly I would like prison.

In the poem, "Now that the time seems all mine," the concept is shaped, as in the author's first poem, by the same instrument of inversion, but the aim here is not to affirm but to deny. The title practically says it all, "now that the time seems all mine," and to complete the title, merely affix the last line, "suddenly I would like prison."

At this point, the poem is obviously accountable for an unresolved area, and as it happens, a crucial one: How does the newly acquired time and freedom (with their catalogue of intricate and pleasurable items made available) relate reasonably with its abrupt rejection in favor of the "prison" which—in apt contrast to the new state of freedom—represents the daily standard portion of constricted time and circumstances?

No explanation is given for the rather cryptic last line, no link forged between the new freedom and its rejection, no clear accounting for the ultimate preference for "prison."

If we may hazard a probable explanation, we see two possible reasons for the rejection. The first is the more easily acceptable, thus: The persona is actually a creature of habits whose life is a routinized set of activities that has developed into a kind of comfortable nest. In other words, the new freedom doesn't make the persona feel "free," and (paraphrasing a Hegelian pronouncement) "the prisoner has learned to love his chains."

The second interpretation seems much more of a "literary insight." We see the persona here as beset daily with routines and impending demands and mandates constantly a-brewing. The pleasures of the new freedom are more keenly enjoyable when inhibited and short-lived: the loosening clouds and prowling cats on the roof are rare sights "caught on the fly," as it were, and such moments stolen from the established "prison" consequently imbue the fleeting pleasures with more intensity and sharpness than when viewed at leisure; the latter is what ironically obtains whenever the unavailable or "forbidden" is suddenly free and permitted and available.

I greatly fancy both of these potential, and valid, interpretations, but the poet has taken a great and improvident risk with this second poem in using such a totally elliptical procedure.

Lacking the metaphorical ballast that is so propitious in fleshing the first poem into wholeness, "this second piece is *actually a group of assertive prose statements, not a poem,*"—the reaction of a certain writer[1] who also observed that the last line "*hovers in air*" without the crucial metaphoric bridge between the pleasurable and its rejection.

Very sharply these two free-verse poems indicate what happens, respectively, with and without the two major requirements of poetic form (the metaphoric structure and the critical tools in operation): either we have a resounding success, or a poaching into prose territory.

Format III. Two examples of well-written contemporary poetry using the traditional style.

Format IIIa. "A Game of Chess," Elizabeth Jennings

Readers and poets in the recently past and recently present centuries used to tick off the traditional poetry of nineteenth century English and American literature as conservative, meaning that the poetry of the period seldom, if ever, ventured from the established patterns and practices, such as rhyme and meter, recognizable rhythmic beat, the use of predesignated symbols, the substance (content) cast into conventional stanza form or into more regularized patterns like the sonnet, villanelle, sestina, quatrain, tercet, etc.

Quite unsettling must have been the advent of free verse in the first third of the twentieth century. Liberation from the established norms greatly flustered poetry's ordered nature; a conspicuous change identifies free verse now with, among others, the more direct articulation of prose statement.

For a while the upbeat style discouraged the use of the traditional format as antiquated and somehow anachronistic and routinary, until lately, when a growing number of established poets started to write poetry in the traditional style while mostly retaining the contemporary manner of utterance, the latter of course using the vocabulary of our time. In the current tracking back to the traditional, a common practice is to adapt or create slightly changed versions of the old features to blend into the current style. But more and more practitioners prefer not to adulterate the traditional format, so that only the presently used diction and a more sophisticated employment of the internal poetry instruments distinguish the refluent format from the old conventional design. A fine example of the practically unadulterated form is "A Game of Chess," written by the eminent contemporary British poet, Elizabeth Jennings.

A Game of Chess

The quiet moves, the gently shaded room:
It is like childhood once again when I
Sat with a tray of toys and you would come
To take my temperature and make me lie
Under the clothes and sleep. Now peacefully

We sit above the intellectual game.
Pure mathematics seems to rule the board
Emotionless. And yet I feel the same
As when I sat and played without a word
Inventing kingdoms where great feelings stirred.

Is it that knight and king and small squat castle
Store up emotion, bring it under rule,
So that the problems now with which we wrestle
Seem simply of the mind? Do feelings cool
Beneath the order of an abstract school?

Never entirely, since the whole thing brings
Me back to childhood when I was distressed:
You seem the same who put away my things
At night, my toys and tools of childish lust.
My king is caught now in a world of trust.

The framework design of "A Game of Chess" is shaped by ordered features of the traditional format: stanzaic and line pattern, rhyme scheme, measured rhythmic beat. Only the voice, its utterance, has the direct-statement quality of current articulating, despite the tone, quietly meditative, that pervades throughout from line to line. Also notable is the inventive use of the internal poetry tools, a feature that distinguishes it from the old tradition's more conventional practice.

What "A Game of Chess" is saying centers on the perennial tension between intellect and emotion, between head and heart; abstraction against intuition, the calculated against the more natural and random ways by which the human personality grows from spontaneous childhood to rational maturity.

Thus, the poem questions: "Do feelings cool/Beneath the order of an abstract school?"—and concludes with its own answer: "Never entirely," considering that the present ambience where the chess game is being played is the very same where as a child, the persona played with her "toys and tools of childhood lust," the little diversions from which the loving and beloved "you" took her away to bed—the same "you" with whom the chess game is now being played. The unchanged situation is a metaphor of unchanging love and confidence kept intact through the years. The poem's metaphoric structure is securely in place.

The internal poetry tools are likewise at work in generating symbols and insights. Among others:

- chess game: the play of intellect
- "Knight and king and small squat castle" storing up emotion and bringing it "under rule": the chess pieces represent the functionaries of the intellect in certain operations, such as in argument, scrutiny, causative reasoning, etc.
- "My king is caught now in a world of trust": a beautiful stratagem of the instrument of inversion
- The use of contrastive juxtaposition underlines the tension between reason and emotion:

  "the problems now with which we wrestle/
  Seem *simply of the mind*" contrasting with:

  "*Inventing kingdoms* where *great feelings* stirred."
  (all italics mine)

The opposite words used, "simply" and "great," are stark and deeply basic words, sharpening the contrast.

- "school": ambivalent word—one, concerning the training and nurture toward maturity; two, a system or body of beliefs or opinions, as in "a school of thought"

The traditional format of the contemporary poem, "A Game of Chess," has demonstrated both poetry indicators put to solid performance.

Format IIIb. "The Impulse," Robert Frost

The free-verse poem following below is another clear example of the contemporary use of the traditional format. "The Impulse" is still one of my favorites among the poems of Robert Frost, the most celebrated poet of America, who enjoyed that distinction throughout his creative lifetime, from the 1920s up to his death in 1963.

Many students have wondered why I consider this poem exemplary, since it lays no claim to resounding eloquence, being rather too casual in tone and delivery. Nonetheless, belying its somewhat homespun patter, it is a work of artistic craftsmanship, carefully ordered and restrained, where the two genre indicators function naturally and inconspicuously.

The crisp beat of the rhythm instantly establishes the impression of regularity and preciseness.

Within the firmly controlled framework of rhyme and meter and substance, the internal poetry instruments are everywhere at work: thematic tension, suggestiveness, ambiguity, understatement, indirection, tone control, among others. Before we go into the specific items that indicate the internal tools in operation, it would be helpful to consider a quotation adapted from an analysis of this poem included in another context.[2]

The Hill Wife
(Retitled: "The Impulse")

It was too lonely for her there,
    And too wild,

And since there were but two of them,
And no child,
And work was little in the house,
She was free,
And followed where he furrowed field,
Or felled tree.
She rested on a log and tossed
The fresh chips,
With a song only to herself
On her lips.
And once she went to break a bough
Of black alder.
She strayed so far she scarcely heard
When he called her—
And didn't answer—didn't speak—
Or return.
She stood, and then she ran and hid
In the fern.
He never found her, though he looked
Everywhere,
And he asked at her mother's house
Was she there.
Sudden and swift and light as that
The ties gave,
And he learned of finalities
Besides the grave.

Here begins the quoted discussion:

Incompatibility between husband and wife provides the occasion for the insight here which may be stated, thus: ***There is a hidden truth deep down things that can only be understood in the world of sensitiveness and the imagination.*** The wife is carefree and childlike; he is completely engrossed in his work, in the everyday routine of the farm. She takes time to enjoy nature; his only concern is to subdue nature to meet his material needs. She senses the distance between them—they never truly "hear" or "see" each other. So that what begins as a game of hide-and-seek on her part ends in her sudden realization of the true meaning of this (initially) playful concealment, that it is really a correlative of the serious lack of communication between them. In other words, that the distance between them is not physical but metaphysical. She cannot be absorbed in the work the way he is, and he simply cannot share in her childlike response to the world of people and of nature—so that when she finally disappears, he follows the most usual and unimaginative procedure in his search: he looks for her at her mother's house.

His wife's disappearance is an unexpected and mysterious incident in his life; it brings him to realize that there are other, subtler truths about human beings apart from the obvious basic truths, that there is a way of living that is more than existence, and a way of dying that is not just the death of the grave. For there is a separation that is worse (more "final") than the separation of actual absence or of death, the separation of people who do not essentially see or hear each other even as they live in close proximity. It is therefore poetic justice for her to disappear since, to all purposes, she has long disappeared from him, anyway.

Here ends the quoted material.

The items that follow below are comments on the functioning of the internal instruments in the poem:

Thematic tension

Ordinarily, thematic tension serves as the hub holding together the bodywork that materializes the poem's meaning; however, in this poem, the thematic tension is just airily defined; no blatant attempt is made to contrastively describe the man and his wife, who are the tensive crux of the whole dramatic situation.

Suggestiveness

Instead, their contrasting natures are suggestively exposed in their daily routines; he, working the fields, and she, done with housework, following him around as he worked, an act suggestive of her childlike nature. Even her playful way with the woodchips, and her singing, are similarly suggestive. She is fanciful, apparently prankish, and with a sprightly imagination.

Ambiguous characterization

Although the whole poem spotlights the wife in that wild and lonely place ("It was too lonely for her there/And too wild"), it turns out that she is not the central character of the poem. Rather, it is the stolid unimaginative husband, since in the end it is he who gets the full impact of the sober truth the poem reveals, as enacted in their little drama: "And he learned of finalities/Besides the grave."

Indirection

The last line of the poem practically announces the theme or meaning, but actually it is not a handout assertion of the poet—it is a typical Frostian maneuver, an "earned" assertion that is evident in many of Frost's more frequently quoted poems. Upon scrutiny, what seems like a prose "statement" ending the poem is really not a statement at all, but is rather an *indirect* (metaphoric) pronouncement of the poem's developed theme or meaning. A *direct* and thorough statement of the theme would be something like this: "Life has other painful terminations besides death; this is a truth among the veritable mine of truths deep down things and can only be understood in the world of sensitiveness and the imagination." Whereas this direct statement has taken thirty-three words to articulate the theme thoroughly and precisely, the last line of this poem takes only nine words to deliver a compact pronouncement because of its indirect way, the way of implication that transfigures the reader's interpretation of the line as his own experience: Mr. Frost's canny metaphorical way of "stating" the poem's meaning makes the reader, in a very private and personal sense, an enhancer and co-creator of the poem.

Symbolic details

- "break"
- "black alder"

There could be a hint of ambiguity in the interpretation of these two symbols. In itself, very telling and unambiguous is the word *break*, and it is chosen here instead of "cut" or "snap off" or "snip" or "hack off" or "clip" or "lop off," for the reason that *break* is clearly more euphoniously suggestive of abrupt disjointing. Much more to the point, *break* does carry definite metaphysical connotations of shattering and critical separation (as in "break a relationship," "break the silence," "break the habit"), where the other possible choices mentioned call up merely *physical* images of detaching.

In "black alder" and its obvious gloomy symbolism a bit of subtle technique is at work. At this point in the poem, the details characterizing the wife show only the light, bright side of her nature; although clearly a deliberate act, the breaking of the "black alder," with its dark symbolism, is not in her psyche at this point—so the symbolism, it appears, is actually meant for the reader as a subliminal anticipatory nudge toward some disastrous revelation or event. This "furtive nudge technique" is this poet's favorite use of the forecaster-symbol, such as the "woodbine leaves" and "woodbine berries" in "Love and a Question," where both symbols anticipate the bridegroom's cautious considering of future bad times; another example is "Good blocks of oak it was I split" in the dynamic poem, "Two Tramps in Mudtime," foreshadowing the "split decision" that the persona would have to make in the end.

Alliteration

The alliterated words contribute toward the characterization of the man and his wife, and ultimately toward the revelation of the poetic meaning.

> "*f*ree"
> "*f*ollowed where he *f*urrowed *f*ield/Or *f*elled tree"
> "The *f*resh chips"
> "**b**reak a **b**ough/Of **b**lack alder"
> "she ran and hid/In the *f*ern"
> "Sudden and swift and light as that/The ties gave/
> And he learned of *f*inalities/Besides the grave."

A quick scrutiny of the words with alliterated sounds shows their role in the presentation of the restrained, the almost muted drama that is the metaphorical embodiment of the theme. However, with "*f*resh chips," the attention is not so much on the initial *f*—since "fresh" is not thematically crucial—but rather of more interest is "chips," which ever so gently anticipates the broken black alder in the next stanza.

Rendered or dramatized symbol

The scene in the fern contains the full theme or meaning of the poem: When the wife ran and hid in the fern, it was her impulsive choice not to answer his call. Deeply hidden in the fern, she found in her sudden invisibility a highly evocative truth about their relationship, about his inability to perceive into depths—specifically, into the depths of her own nature. Of course we are to assume that this realization came as more of an intuitional rather than a rational awareness on her part, together with her implicit acknowledgment that his own honest garden-variety sort of nature is equipped with only the "outward eye," with no depth of recognition.

For her part, as the reader could see, she did try to "perceive" him in her own way, following him around as he went about his work, for it seemed the only companionable sharing allowed her by the constricted circumstances and routines. But she did make the attempt to "see" him—and the point is, he himself had not thought of so "perceiving" her. All this must have passed as a flash of instinctive awareness. The little drama in the enclosing fern, and its resolution, quite crushing, if instinctive, is the moment of truth for her. For the reader, the little scene is a compact correlative of the covert separatedness and could serve as a dramatized symbol, its intensity and power lurking and inherent in the way of all symbols.

Moment of illumination

- "And he asked at her mother's house/Was she there."

For both reader and persona, this final act of searching by the persona is revelatory; it is so symptomatic of the predictable and obvious recourse. (Where does one ultimately look for a young runaway wife?)

For the reader: appreciation of the poet's subtle craftsmanship. In underlining the persona's predictable and unimaginative act, the poet has gently clinched his characterization of the persona as a rather dumpy, unimaginative man.

For the persona: His fruitless search and his loss bring a sudden illumination of other cruel losses "besides the grave." Because his plain and simple thinking had not reckoned that his wife's fanciful impulsive flight would take her anywhere else than (predictably!) to her mother's house, his discovery of other "terminations" is a costly disclosure.

"The Impulse" is a demonstration of tight poetic control, a quick but incisive evidence that "carefree-versing" into prose territory can be controlled through the discipline required in the use of traditional limits like rhyme and meter and regularized rhythm—considering, of course, that the two genre indicators are also judiciously in place.

Format IV. Traditionally disposed contemporary poetry without the metaphoric structure. Included here is a fine example that uses the metaphor frame.

Format IVa. "The Leaden-Eyed," Vachel Lindsay

Expectedly, some poems that are disposed to the traditional style, whether contemporary or poems of the recent past, are careful to keep the external features of rhyme pattern and meter scheme and recognizable rhythmic beat, among other traditional features, and to otherwise present them as duly crafted components of the traditional in scrupulous form—yet it often happens that altogether forgotten is the required metaphorical structure. Consequently, the mechanical form is in place, but the substance ends up stating (*rather than rendering*) its pellet of meaningfulness, leaving the reader with nothing to do except swallow the handout. Thus: "Tell me not in mournful numbers/Life is but an empty dream/For the soul is dead that slumbers"; and "So live that when thy summons comes to join/The innumerable caravan, which moves/To that mysterious realm .../Thou go not, like the quarry slave, etc." The reader is regaled by the eloquence and the euphony and musicality. Like many readers, I still retain, in fact, my young enthusiastic response to the grandeur of the "Thanatopsis" theme and its rolling eloquence. But with any eloquent poem that lacks the metaphoric rendering, the reader is not given the opportunity to enhance the poem for a fuller enjoyment through his own imaginative response to the evocations forged by internal poetry instruments. In "The Leaden-Eyed," these hardly operate, such artistic tools as suggestiveness, tone shifts, and inventive word usages, among other creative tools intrinsic to the metaphoric procedure.

The Leaden-Eyed

Let not the young souls be smothered out before
They do quaint deeds and fully flaunt their pride.
It is the world's one crime its babes grow dull,
Its poor are ox-like limp and leaden-eyed.

Not that they starve, but starve so dreamlessly;
Not that they sow, but that they seldom reap;
Not that they serve, but have no gods to serve;
Not that they die, but that they die like sheep.

A trenchant comment on the deprived people of society, "The Leaden-Eyed" is persuasive and forceful, though more as a deprecatory statement than as a poem in traditional form. But it is also evident that the use of a certain artistic technique lends to its easy and persuasive reading; however, although this technique is used with subtle and intricate obliquity, it does not generate the more creative touch that richly enhances the total articulation, and the reason is easy to see.

The absence of inventive word usages and fresh insights, the lack of connotative images and other suggestive details that indicate the internal poetic instruments at work, account for the fact that the theme of the poem, its meaning, is more *stated* than given shape by dramatic situations and symbolic images. The verses are actually direct statements of the poem's meaning, eloquently and euphoniously uttered but virtually declarative prose statements.

Consequently rhetorical in effect are the series of contrastive/ confirmative parallelisms: "***Not that*** they (starve, sow, serve, die) ***but*** ..."; these parallels are deftly executed with a certain interesting bit of intricacy, but even this strategy cannot compensate for the lack of metaphoric structuring.

To explain the intricacy in the parallelisms: Usually following the first half of the contrastive parallel is the expected component-half that fulfills the contrast signaled by "***but*** ..." Thus, in the first parallelism: "not that they starve, ***but*** ..." what expectedly follows could be a word or words in contrast to "starve"; instead, "starve" is repeated, not to negate or minimize or contradict, but most surprising and suitable, ***to introduce a new concept***, "dreamlessly," a very pertinent concept that instead ***affirms*** and ***enhances*** the picture of starving. Decidedly not usual—but easy and acceptable—is this rather inventive "violation" of the contrastive parallel's standard formula. The rest of the parallels follow suit in this turn that discomposes the contrastive "bite" of ***but*** and manipulates it instead into a more or less confirmative instrument in the poem. Simple but ingenious is the twisting of antithesis into synthesis.

Of course, the word "just" or "only" could have been affixed, thus: "Not *just* that ...," "Not *only* that ...," and the import of the parallelisms is quickly made clear—but this would have given the whole game away.

Parenthetically, this is not to diminish the effectiveness of parallelism as a literary tool. The most eloquent and adhesive to one's memory are the parallel verses of St. Paul in his gospel-letters, and the innumerable contrastive parallels in the Book of Proverbs.

Most direct and telling are the parallelisms in the parables of Jesus; foremost in memory are the disparities in the two parallel houses built respectively on rock and on sand—and the parable ending with the shrewdly unparalleled "... and great was the fall of it."

For eloquent and proclamatory articulation, parallelism is a surefire instrument, but it often seems more compelling as a whizzbang weapon of rhetoric.

For the rest, some words like the stolid descriptive "ox-like" and the humans dying "like sheep" could perhaps do with a more suggestive and insightful rendition, using the procedure familiarly belonging within the proper metaphorical framework that is sorely missing here.

Format IVb. "The Golf Links," Sarah N. Cleghorn

In contrast to the foregoing poem, "The Golf Links" by Sarah N. Cleghorn shows how the metaphorical structuring can keep a traditional format from articulating in prose.

The poem consists of four short lines, a concise demonstration of a framework almost impeccably structured in metaphor, and incisively shaped up by the internal instruments of inversion, contrast-by-juxtaposition, ironic tone, suggestiveness, and understatement.

The Golf Links

The golf links lie so near the mill
    That almost every day
The laboring children can look out
    And see the men at play.

Like "The Leaden-Eyed," the above poem is in traditional format, and asserts the same theme of censure against the plight of the socially disadvantaged. However, this little poem of four lines makes the point casually but with devastating sharpness.

Two sets of disparities are all the poem needs to expose a scandalous scenario and mount an incisive condemnation in an ever-so-gentle satiric understatement. The two sets of disparities that yoke "golf links" and "mill," and "laboring children" and "men at play" pack an explosive that could discomfit an equal number of ardent parallelisms such as those we find in "The Leaden-Eyed."

Sound, be it eloquent or not, is predictable, it announces itself. But, as in "The Golf Links," is there anything more awesome than resonance begotten of silence?

Format IVc. "The Conqueror Worm," Edgar Allan Poe

The poem by Robert Frost, "The Impulse," has demonstrated that the discipline in using the external limits of the traditional format is equally responsible with the internal instruments in keeping free verse from the "too-free" tendency. However, the poem by Vachel Lindsay also shows that, despite adherence to the ordered limits of the traditional framework, a poem is artistically hamstrung by the lack of metaphoric structuring.

About the poem below, "The Conqueror Worm" by Edgar Allan Poe, it is somehow reassuring to poetry writers that even a proclaimed traditional poet could misuse the metaphoric structuring.

The Conqueror Worm

Lo! 'tis a gala night
    Within the lonesome latter years
An angel throng, bewinged, bedight
    In veils, and drowned in tears,
Sit in a theater to see
    A play of hopes and fears,
While the orchestra breathes fitfully
    The music of the spheres.

Mimes, in the form of God on high,
    Mutter and mumble low,
And hither and thither fly—
    Mere puppets they, who come and go
At bidding of vast formless things
    That shift the scenery to and fro,
Flapping from out their Condor wings
    Invisible Wo.

That motley drama—oh, be sure
    It shall not be forgot!
With its Phantom chased for evermore
    By a crowd that seize it not,
Through a circle that ever returneth in
    To the self-same spot,
And much of Madness, and more of Sin,
    And Horror the soul of the plot.

But see amid the mimic rout
    A crawling shape intrude!
A blood-red thing that writhes from out
    The scenic solitude!
It writhes!—it writhes!—with mortal pangs
    The mimes become its food,
And seraphs sob at vermin fangs
    In human gore imbued.

Out—out are the lights—out all!
    And, over each quivering form,
The curtain, a funeral pall,
    Comes down with the rush of a storm,
While the angels, all pallid and wan,

Uprising, unveiling, affirm
That the play is the tragedy, "Man,"
And its hero, the Conqueror Worm.

There could be several ways in which the metaphorical framework of a poem might go awry; in "The Leaden-Eyed," it is altogether missing, leaving the field to what amounts to prose statements.

However, on the other hand, "The Conqueror Worm" is initially seen as metaphorically structured because of the obviously symbolic images and the representative characters acting out the theme on the theater stage. Nevertheless, a studious look reveals that the poem's so-called metaphoric frame is actually an erroneous contrivance, a non-operational shortcut of the more stringent demands of creative metaphoring.

The aberrant structure is discovered by a careful look at two aspects: first, at the *substance* of the poem and its designed meaning which may be summarized, thus: "Human life is essentially tragic. Beset by travail, the earthly henchmen of God are held futile, being themselves blown about by the ill winds of 'Invisible Wo' (Woe). And soon Death, aptly symbolized as a Worm, promptly conquers and devours every mortal remains."

The second aspect, needing a closer attention, is the *form*.

Expectedly, this poem in traditional format is consistently rhymed and metered. The five stanzas, according to the critic C. W. Kent,[3] correspond properly to the five Acts of a tragic play, not just because of the tragic theme, but mainly because the contrived metaphoric frame specifies a theater, where the theme is scrupulously dramatized by the symbolized characters. By these symbolic appearances the poem is initially seen to be suitably and precisely structured metaphorically. Moreover, in the symbolizing process the device of inversion has properly cast a *worm* as the *conqueror.*

With all the symbolizing, however, the substance of the poem is itself not placed in symbolic form, and this "stated" unmetaphored substance is the instrument cobbling the poem's improper framework, where none of the symbolized characters and details function as authentic metaphors, for this reason: these crucial details are presented as mere *symbol-namings* of themselves, as in these unmetaphored "name-symbols": *Invisible Wo, Madness, Sin, Horror.* The only metaphor-symbols which do not outright appear as their own "symbolized" selves are the "mimes," assigned to represent "God on high" (who is cast as ineffective), and the other is "Phantom," representing the ideal state or condition that the depicted human crowd vainly chases and is never able to grasp. Just those two are metaphors, the rest are mere "name-symbols" of themselves.

In other words, the framework is more allegory than metaphor. Being allegory, it lacks the freshness of new and inventive insights into the viscera, of human pathos.

Obviously, therefore, the whole substance could have been properly built into a true metaphoric structure, say, a situation *analogously* portraying the tragic progression of human life—something commonly used perhaps, like a land trip or a sea voyage marked by storm and other distressing events, and giving these familiar metaphorical situations an uncommon and original fleshly treatment as, for instance, in Ophelia Dimalanta's "On a Slow Boat to Bohol." Or there is challenge in other analogues, invented or less commonly used.

The prudent craftsman knows that his poem navigates in the same symbolical area as the allegory, the fable, and the parable, and is careful to steer by the more inventive metaphorical procedure of poetry.

Format IVd. "The Murdered Traveller," William Cullen Bryant

The nineteenth-century poem, "Thanatopsis" by William Cullen Bryant, is more familiar and more highly regarded than "The Murdered Traveller," written by the same author, but we prefer to use the latter here because "Thanatopsis," although a resounding memorable work, is much too long a piece and too ponderous for our purpose of demonstration.

The poem below is clearly traditional in format.

The Murdered Traveller

When Spring, to woods and wastes around,
    Brought bloom and joy again,
The murdered traveller's bones were found,
    Far down a narrow glen.

The fragrant birch, above him, hung
    Her tassels in the sky;
And many a vernal blossom sprung,
    And nodded careless by.

The redbird warbled, as he wrought
    His hanging nest o'er head,

And fearless, near the fatal spot,
    Her young the partridge led.

But there was weeping far away,
    And gentle eyes, for him,
With watching many an anxious day,
    Were sorrowful and dim.

They little knew, who loved him so,
    The fearful death he met,
When shouting o'er the desert snow,
    Unarmed, and hard beset;—

Nor how, when round the frosty pole
    The northern dawn was red,
The mountain wolf and wildcat stole
    To banquet on the dead;—

Nor how, when strangers found his bones,
    They dressed the hasty bier,
And marked his grave with nameless stones,
    Unmoistened by a tear.

But long they looked, and feared, and wept,
    Within his distant home;
And dreamed, and started as they slept,
    For joy that he was come.

Long, long they looked—but never spied
    His welcome step again,
Nor knew the fearful death he died
    Far down that narrow glen.

A third way the metaphoric structure could go subtly awry is evident in "The Murdered Traveller." It adheres strictly to the limits of rhyme, rhythm, meter, and rhythmic beat, the constituents that immediately make for its easy and expressive reading. However, despite these firmly controlled elements, a more demanding aspect to consider is the indecisive use here of poetic tension, which is actually the potential hub holding this poem together.

The opening three stanzas immediately set up a tensive contrast between the world of nature flourishing in the tide of springtime, on the one hand, and on the other, the barren spot where the murdered man's bones have been buried by the hands of strangers. Meticulous details and images of nature develop and expand the contrast, which is further emphasized by the conspicuous juxtaposition of the two contrary elements of springtime and death, thus: the nest of the warbling redbird hangs over the grave and the partridge leads her young flock "near the fatal spot."

The emotional tension produced by these contrasts serves to prepare for the thematic tension that is evoked in the final six stanzas. The last stanzas focus on the dead man's grieving and unknowing family "weeping far away," and also mention the fearful manner of his death. In the use of contrast, an interesting variant may be noted about the divergent role of nature, both as simple contrastive/ironic instrument, and as gluttonously savage—"the mountainwolf and wildcat" that "stole/To banquet on the dead."

Despite the profuse aura of tension, however pervasive, the poem misses out on the crucial function of this artistic instrument: no attention is given to the tension generated by the distance between the bereaved and the beloved dead, no attempt to define the relevances in "*But there was weeping far away*" as well as in the family's condition of unknowing. These are the obvious factors that could raise the whole poetic stance from simple straight narrative to metaphorical meaningfulness.

In the line quoted above, the obvious working words are "But" and "far away." The initial "But" signals the tension that is potentially productive of the meaning and significance of the separation.

It is now obvious that what is responsible for the lack of attention on the pivotal factors of distance and the state of unknowing is the fact that the narrated material remains at the narrative level. A sad and ironic story is told and the reaction evoked is simply emotional rather than a response to an experience that has significance. Clearly, the story needs a theme or meaning that explains: What does the whole event mean besides the usual ironic and emotional response it elicits? What underlying truth or truths are signified by this event, where the strong emotive factors lie in the condition of distance, separation, and unknowing?

Our purpose here is only demonstrative, it is not to rewrite a poem to specifications. The following suggestions for potential themes are meant just to show that a case like the present one can generate a relevant truth for its theme. From the tensive elements involved a meaningful idea can emerge, such as: "The interrelated condition of distance, separation, and unknowing is two-edged; it is a matter of weeping but also a matter of hope that keeps the dead 'alive' as long as the sad condition exists or is not discarded." This suggested theme posits a solid poetic paradox.

Another meaningful truth, but perhaps rather more unwieldy for this poem, is—if I may be pardoned—something borrowed from one of my very earliest poems, thus: "The loss is gain for the will to choose/The distance-given right to know"; in other words, the privilege, beyond emotion, for the "dear embracing brute embrace/

Of reason shocking ..."—the choice for reason to acknowledge the beloved dead as indeed dead.

In all our discussions so far on the various Formats, our ultimate objective is neither to show up or applaud but merely to demonstrate. "The Murdered Traveller" presents one of the stances manifested in the Romantic tradition, so that we may perhaps not even expect a further performance beyond the narrative-emotional procedure it has taken.

What we have undertaken is to show a third example of how a traditional poetic structure may be raised from a direct narrative-or-statement level to a metaphorical experience that renders its theme or meaning, which is after all the core item expected of every good literary offering.

Format V. The first of the three poems included here represents good poetry writing, but it is what may be called "could-have-been-great." The two others, free-verse poems, demonstrate the use of the "ingredient missing" in the first poem.

Format Va. "The Rhodora," Ralph Waldo Emerson

We find that many a fine traditional poem written in the nineteenth century tends to rest its ultimate appeal on eloquence and euphoniousness, thus often leaving its substance in need of thematic enrichment, of some highlighting idea or ideas that could be generated from a purposive use of poetry's enriching internal instruments.

Yet, quite often a well-written poem in the traditional style receives a faster reader response than a free-verse counterpart, granting that they both deal with the same subject. Understandably in this matter, the traditional format has the quicker advantage in its musicality, in the appealing ordered beat of rhythm and rhyme. However, a traditional poem, well-written but with a needful substance, misses the leap to the accolade of "great," and is undoubtedly "good but could-have-been." Of course, the leap is no easy doing, and its demands are apparently not even in the usual working practice of the period in which the poem was written.

Examples are three poems following below: "The Rhodora" by Ralph Waldo Emerson, and two recent free-verse poems, "Afternoon Gardener" by Alfred A. Yuson and "Gladiolus and Her Kind" by Ernesto S. Yee, who is a poet quite attuned to musical influence, being also a concert pianist.

Very reassuring to poetry writers is to see that the great American poet-philosopher Emerson has written a poem that could demonstrably need some augmenting of its substance. "The Rhodora" shows how a fine outstanding poem could miss its greatness and fullness.

The Rhodora

In May, when sea-winds pierced our solitudes,
I found the fresh Rhodora in the woods,
Spreading its leafless blooms in a damp nook,
To please the desert and the sluggish brook.
The purple petals, fallen in the pool,
Made the black water with their beauty gay;
Here might the redbird come his plumes to cool,
And court the flower that cheapens his array.

Rhodora! if the sages ask thee why
This charm is wasted on the earth and sky,
Tell them, dear, that if eyes were made for seeing,
Then Beauty is its own excuse for being:
Why thou wert there, O rival of the rose!
I never thought to ask, I never knew:
But, in my simple ignorance, suppose
The selfsame Power that brought me there brought you.

"The Rhodora" has several potential opportunities for resonating and enriching itself. To begin with, the content or substance develops an impelling primal theme which may be stated as follows: "Humankind is intrinsically in harmonious and spiritual affinity with the natural world." It is a theme magnificent and expansive enough to contain several relatedly important corollaries that could magnify the substance.

Of course, such corollaries are not meant as extended developments in the poetic structure, they are meant simply to *resonate*, and thus provide enhancement for the central concept or theme, as for the theme defined above.

A related concept that could be evoked in this poem by more purposive use of poetry's internal instruments is: the idea that both the human creature and his world are not only fashioned by the same Creator but are also propelled by His power: "The selfsame Power that *brought me there* brought you" (italics mine). What meaningful and significant evocations may vibrate in the idea of 'divine propulsion'? What is it like to be God-driven? Reverberating this idea through suggestiveness or inventive diction or the use of tension or other internal tools could surely enhance the main concept.

Another potential corollary idea explores a more intimate insight into the relationship between the man-persona and his world. Unless the Rhodora flower (representing the natural world of man) is equipped with the same or similar vocable sensibilities as the man, the man-flower relationship is posited absolutely on human presumption and awareness alone. For a further insight into the relationship, the poem could perhaps motivate the man's attitude to convey the hierarchy—or whatever other nub—that further defines the relationship.

These purely demonstrative examples or any others that could enlarge the poetic substance do not require extended treatment in the structure, for the intention is just the toned-down reverberation of related concepts to magnify the assertion of the poem.

Format Vb. "Afternoon Gardener," Alfred A. Yuson

Being shorn of the ordered musicality of the traditional poetry format, free verse could be shorter on a quick reader-reception—but could be longer on the enhanced substance, and as with all good poetry, also on capturing the slower but more rewarding scrutiny of the reader. Generally, traditional poems of the nineteenth century are steeped in profound and encompassing themes; today, good poetry, in free verse or otherwise, is challenged to invest even the familiar and the manifestly trivial with complexity and with inventive strokes in the craftsmanship, as in the poem below, "Afternoon Gardener" by Alfred A. Yuson.

Afternoon Gardener

For him, depth is unbecoming.
He'd rather stare down the measure
of brown road
into the green froth of hills beginning
and the finite blue of finished mountains.

He takes his coffee levelled,
musing about ants
and what he regards
as their honest dimensions.

Someday he'd come right off the ground
he works and waters in familiar
genuflection, Come right off and crawl
down the measure of brown road,
Crawl right off from his prayers
With a teaspoon and a hoe,
Into the finite green and the beginning blue.

The best free verse written today makes copious and arresting use of the internal instruments of poetry and in so doing, turns out pieces marked by: one, weighty poetic substance enriched by nuances and complexities; and two, the craftsmanship subtly extending the word to its full semantic operation in its context. In the display of these two qualities, "Afternoon Gardener" is a generic representative.

The main concept of the poem centers on defining the gardener-persona's attitude toward the "high" and the "low" in life, the exalted and the lowly. These polar conditions are variously depicted in terms of images and situations generated in the course of the gardener-persona's introspection. The author portrays the persona's thoughts in a sequence that develops the subtle turns and modulations in this interesting character's introspection, the author using internal poetry devices that crucially evoke the covert and sophistic sensibilities of the gardener.

The persona's introspection betrays furtive equivocal attitudes moving from a preferment for the lowly, and shifting to a hankering for the "elevated," leaving his lowly employment for the distant heights—only to end with a fugitive but unmistakable avowal for his present humble state.

The pithy structure portrays a play-down of high priorities, with the reduction carried out in a crafty fashion that actually magnifies the minimals into their "honest dimensions." As in a number of Yuson's pieces, this particular poem fairly swarms with the evocative words and phrases and details arising from his use of the internal poetry instruments.

The first stanza announces the persona's minimal choices—for him, no profundities ("depth is unbecoming"); for him, just the comfort of casual introspecting such as he finds in the apparently random contemplating on his geographical context, which is depicted among others by details fraught with minimizing connotations:

> "*measure* of brown road"
>
> "hills *beginning*"
>
> "*finite* blue of finished mountains" (all italics mine)

The second stanza's very first line, "He takes his coffee levelled," not only repeats the lowly stance, it turns to account the unmistakable allusion to the pensive self-deprecation of J. Alfred Prufrock: "*I have measured out my life with coffee spoons.*"

In the third stanza, the persona declares his decision to leave the gardener's work that literally bows him down in a constant posture of humility ("in familiar genuflection"), and to take to the road and thence to the far mountains and their challenging heights.

However, in a deft "camouflaging" maneuver, the poem ends with a seeming apostasy by the gardener's avowing his choice for the lower stance. This reductive choice is intimated in a number of critically functional words, phrases, and details that bear the stamp of their origin from the operation of internal poetry tools:

> "someday" — By this word the momentous resolve (to leave for the heights) is reduced to the merely hypothetical.
>
> "crawl" — The persona will not leave with head held high, but will *crawl* off the measure of brown road.
>
> "stare down" — An idiom that denigrates the ambivalent "measure of brown road."
>
> "teaspoon" and "hoe" — When he leaves for the heights he will take with him these minimal/minimizing implements of his present employment.

Now for the two final *coups de main*. The very first line of the poem goes:

> "For him depth is unbecoming."

In this line, as well as in the following lines up to and including all four lines of the second stanza, "depth" stands for profundities, for intellectual superiority, which the persona considers unbecoming, particularly for him. Yet, *depth* also stands essentially and materially for the low levels (i. e., the low levels are also unbecoming), so that the word, being ambivalently operative, dredges up the persona's equivocal attitude.

The final revelation is done in a variant but graceful replication of the following line, thus:

> "the finite blue of finished mountains" (in the first stanza)
> "the finite green and the beginning blue" (last line)

The first line repeated like an echo at the end of the poem telescopes the persona's true attitude to end where he began—the preference is to remain in the humble state. The repetition makes superfluous any buildup to their richly involuted conclusion.

Very clearly, the poem confirms the fact that the direct statement (prose) burgeons into poetry when articulated with the use of the following internal poetry instruments—ambivalence, inversion, allusion, tone control, and repetition, among others—that make for the opulence and subtlety and complexity of the piece.

Format Vc. "Gladiolus and Her Kind," Ernesto S. Yee

Gladiolus and Her Kind

Out in the green or in a jug full of water,
Your sword-shaped leaves parry
Midsummer air and your spikes disarm
With ribands flame-red, gold, and the creamy
White dove feathers.

Old as Africa, Europe and Asia,
Your opulent corms
Gifted by Grandmother's
Patient green thumb hoard her love
For the brilliant and the quiet.
My gorgeous giver of gladness,

You, too, receive my adoration:
From the jug where you now stand
Your land of silence offers
The glow of colors,
Your long, leafy stems tilt
Over, each one miming a beloved's waist
Leaning to catch my murmur of thanks.
Beauty need not speak.

Even a fast reading of "Gladiolus and Her Kind" discovers that its theme or concept is intensified and the poetic substance expanded. The intensifying and expanding result from the muted vibrations of certain related sensations and ideas.

Starting from the first stanza the poem is held tightly together by the poetic tension generated in the pairing of mutually disparate acts and details:

- disparate textures evoked by the "*sword*-shaped leaves parry(ing)/Midsummer *air*" (italics mine)
- the flower's "spikes disarm" with their fiery colors and "creamy/White dove feathers"
- the juxtaposition of large and remote influences, "Africa, Europe and Asia" with "Grandmother's/Patient green thumb"
- the pairing of the "brilliant" (loud) with the "quiet" (soundless/motionless): synaesthetic seeing and hearing
- the joining of geographical distance and metaphysical nearness, the *macro* subsumed by the *micro*: "From the jug where you now stand/Your land of silence offers ..."

- the "long, lovely stems" that "tilt/Over" juxtaposed with their personalized identities, each stem "miming a beloved's waist/Leaning ..."
- The final disparity (which is the central concept or theme) proclaims the reality of Beauty made available ("audible") even through silence: "Beauty need not speak."

These related ideas and sensations reverberate throughout the structure and paradoxically, the spreading-out and expansion do not dilute or disperse the impact of the poetic substance; a good scrutiny confirms that the content is rendered even more solid and compact.

About magnifying the substance with related ideas and sensations, the obvious keyword is *reverberate*; not obtrusive presence but the "silent" and potent vibrations work the magic of enlargement.

"The Rhodora," a memorable traditional poem of profound meaning as it is, misses the opportunity for augmentation, its greatness a peak that remains potential. This is not at all to minimize the poem which the dynamic author wrote in the conventions of the period that did not lay special stress on the heightened-but-restrained language and resonant complexities integral in the poetry of today. In the two unassuming free-verse poems, the related ideas and sensations confirm that the respective structures have not missed the opportunities for enlargement.

Format VI. A variant procedure of free verse by the adoption of traditional elements in its format.

Format VIa. "The Innocence of Solomon," Nick Joaquin

A growing number of free-verse poems are being written today using various constituents of the traditional format such as rhyme and meter, and some preferred conventional stanza patterns like the sonnet and variations of the couplet, tercet, or quatrain. These "reclaimed" traditional features undoubtedly enhance the free-verse format, but only as far as the external requisites go; actually, in themselves these traditional features do not authenticate the poetry piece—unless the substance is also developed by metaphorical rendering and by the purposive operation of internal poetry tools. Lacking these two poetry indicators, free verse, with or without traditional features, expectedly articulates in virtual prose.

With all this, it cannot be denied that the traditional features being reclaimed really help to keep the free verse within bounds; the distinctly poetic earmarks like rhyme and rhythm somehow restrain the general prosiness that could otherwise precipitate the free-verse structure into the prose terrain. Furthermore, these traditional features do infuse an impression of orderliness into the liberated free-verse bodywork.

The following four contemporary poems show the happy impact of ordered elements like rhyme, meter, and conventional stanza patterns blended into the free-verse structure.

To recall a bit of literary history: the first third of the twentieth century ushered in the *vers libre* and the Imagist movements. Relatedly,

"The Innocence of Solomon," written by the late National Artist for Literature Nick Joaquin in 1937, shows that he is one of the earliest, most aware and knowledgeable practitioners of free verse in our country.

The Innocence of Solomon

Sheba, Sheba, open your eyes!
The apes defile the ivory temple,
the peacocks chant dark blasphemies;
but I take your body for mine to trample,
I laugh where once I bent the knees.
Yea, I take your mouth for mine to crumple,
drunk with the wisdom of your flesh.

But wisdom never was content
And flesh when ripened falls at last:
What will I have when the seasons mint
Your golden breasts into golden dust?

Let me arise and follow the river
back to its source: I would bathe my bones
among the chaste rivulets that quiver
out of the clean primeval stones.
Yea, bathe me again in the early vision
my soul tongued forth before your mouth
made of a kiss a fierce contrition
salting the waters of my youth ...

Sheba, Sheba, close my eyes!
The apes have ravished the inner temple,
the peacocks rend the sacred veil
and on the manna feast their fill—
but chaliced drowsily in your ample
arms, with each brief bliss that dies
my own deep sepulcher I seal.

Although the poem, "The Innocence of Solomon," is addressed to the Queen of Sheba, it is actually a meditative soliloquy that dramatizes the sovereign tension between the body and the spirit.

In the mechanical design of the poem, the preponderant number of lines have the beginning word cast in the lower case, at that early stage of free verse in our midst (1937), a seemingly aberrant feature that quickly marked the poem as free verse. On the other hand, the rhymed lines and the strong metrical beat are most conspicuous features of the entire format.

Regarding the beginning word in lower case, what appeared then as a somewhat impious breach of poetry-mechanics must have made for a beguiling innovation to readers; nevertheless, the poem rests its immediate appeal on the substance itself which, to put it euphemistically, is preoccupied with details of fleshly plenitude.

Yet, despite the ecstatic celebration of sensual delights, despite the lavish attention on the fervidly carnal, a haunting aura of pathos pervades the whole poem, a diffusive sadness arising from the crucial loss of the sacred and the holy:

> The apes defile the ivory temple,
> the peacocks chant dark blasphemies;

And the modified repetition of the following two lines, and the added third line deploring the final desecration:

> The apes have ravished the inner temple,
> the peacocks rend the sacred veil
> and on the manna feast their fill—

It is divinity lost in a heedless and heartless fashion which the poet-author has astutely marked as innocence, not guilty, just inevitable, Solomon's vaunted wisdom negating and not in unknowing folly; for it is the deterioration and wasting of the numinous essence that ennobles the human's spirit, if not also his earthly frame. Well the persona knows it as he bewails its loss:

> ... I would bathe my bones
> among the chaste rivulets that quiver
> out of the clean primeval stones.
> Yea, bathe me again in the early vision
> my soul tongued forth ...

The euphonious articulation of the whole poem is controlled by the lyricism and rhythmic beat, elements often extraneous to a free-verse utterance. Further, the substance of the poem is vibrant with the "poeticisms" and philosophical pronouncements attributed to the sovereign wisdom and poetical disposition that begot the Song of Songs—characteristics which the poet-author provided pointedly as crucial components:

> But wisdom never was content
> and flesh when ripened falls at last:
> what will I have when the seasons mint
> your golden breasts into golden dust?
>
> ****
>
> ... before your mouth
> made of a kiss a fierce contrition

The two mutually disparate words in the phrase "fierce contrition" are appropriately forced into union, suggesting the persona's nippy condition of ambivalence and tension between his body and his soul—

"fierce" as his body's ravishment, and "contrition" as the consequent spiritual abasement, both strong disparate emotional states couched in the two words welded compactly in a kiss.

Further: "But chaliced drowsily in your ample/arms, ...

Note the word "chaliced," participially "verbing it with nouns," so to speak, and merging here not only two separate grammatical categories but also two emotional disparities as well. The merging of the flesh and the spirit, as intimated in the physical embracing that is identified as being "chaliced," proclaims the tragedy of the created human being's divided nature.

Ordinarily, when the poetic substance involves a pejorative concept, the utterance is in keeping with the harsh import of the material. This poem does proclaim a pejorative idea, it is an apostasy, but the whole tone is at variance because the articulation is by turns exhilarated and delighted, and lyrical and gently meditative. The sharp discrepancy between idea and tone is relevant as a kind of correlative to the thematic tension.

Furthermore, despite the lyric lilt and the exuberant attention on the bodily delights, the pathos of loss hovers around the whole apostatizing experience, pathos that in the end sinks into tragedy as the persona, ensconced in the "chalice-embrace," accepts the Pyrrhic cost of his self-betrayal, so:

> ... with each brief bliss that dies
> my own deep sepulcher I seal.

As a free-verse poem, "The Innocence of Solomon" is sturdily metaphorical, and likewise makes judicious use of the internal poetry devices; in this poem we have seen in effective operation the instruments of inventive diction, inversion, paradox, and tone control, among others.

The poem is an ample demonstration of how a free-verse poem using aspects of the supplanted traditional format (in this poem, rhyme both slant and exact, and a strong metrical beat) can have nothing to lose and everything to gain in its shaping as a work of art.

Format VIb. "Rain in Granite Country," Edith L. Tiempo

While engaged in the diverse process of creating, the poet is predictably faced with choices and decisions; later, the shrewdest critic has no way of tracing the impulse or reason that motivated this or that particular strategy in the finished work. Unless the explanation is internally evidenced, it is bootless to try.

In the same way, unless critically germane and made evident, whatever impulse or reason motivates a free-verse writer to adopt certain limiting traditional elements into his delimited format can concern no ferreting reader or critic; the choice remains an elusive affair between the poet and the material. Critical judgment may only theorize on the pro and con of such "tinctured" free-verse formats; and often, neither may the poet himself account for the arcane decision that incited the blending—except for the just claim that the finished poem accounts for itself.

Rain in Granite Country

Thirst sometimes comes as a surprise,
It is the thirst
You see in the faces in the schoolroom
Whenever stirred by insight or surmise,
Or recognition still half-puzzles
Like reflections in a dark room;
The other thirst inflicted by the arid air
Everywhere is a latent saboteur,
It's in the parched hibiscus as it bursts
Into posture and color in the drizzles,
It's in the ferns and wild azaleas,
And the stiff and dusty zinnias
Turning sleek in the evening dew.

And suddenly you see
You are in granite country,
And all the while it is your thirst alone
Exploring for moisture like a lizard's tongue
Under root and stone,
Under fallen bamboo,
Into roach and gopher crevices, among
The piles of pitted rocks—
(And those great granite pocks
Never brim over with rain-shower wetness.)

All is semi-dryness
Except for the sensuous
Freshness rushing among the pebbles
Of your mind; in that heady terrain
The waters leap and gurgle and flow
And gush upon the plains outside,
Letting you know
It is always your own rain
That quenches the countryside.

There is perhaps a fair hunk of truth in the assertion that any "well-wrote" poem is a revelation of the human psyche, as revealed by exposition or implication in the finished poem. There is no doubt, however, that a good number of "well-wrought" poems do celebrate certain human attributes, and even sometimes with the poems turning into ars poetica affirmations.

"Rain in Granite Country" may not posit an ars poetica but it does take a human attribute for its theme: *The thirst for experience is intrinsic in the human sensibility.*

In this poem, the internal poetry instruments are not in any remarkable operation, some alliterations here and there, a half-hearted pun, at least one word in fine ambivalence. Rather, the poem owes its easy readability mostly to the unobtrusive oral and aural benefits produced by the rhymings and the rhythmic beat (though the cadence is a bit too sober and mannerly!) and the emotional evocations generated by the images of nature, in particular, by the details of aridity and searing.

But the poem does have something unusual to commend it: By a (somewhat impertinent!) strategic turn, its metaphorical structure is crafted as a *metaphorical inversion.*

This inverted procedure involves the thematic concept and its development:

> *The thirst for experience is intrinsic*
> *in the human sensibility.*

Obviously, in the development of this theme, two operative words are "thirst" and "human sensibility." In the usual or regular process, the thirst [for experience] as indicated here belongs intrinsically to the persona, who then slakes his thirst through the agency of forces *outside* and *inside* of himself.

However, the actual utterance of the poem reverses the regular situation, where the thirst belongs instead to the parched and sapless objects of nature, and in the end it is the persona's own rain coming from the freshness and lively waters of his mind that always "quenches the [dry] countryside."

And yet, despite the inversion, the total revelation of the poem does fulfill the terms of the thematic idea, *as if revealed through the regular, not the inverted, process* that is actually taken by the poem. For, in the ultimate revelation, the persona's thirst is indeed satisfied in the inverted order, where incongruously it is his mind's waters and freshness that quench not *his* thirst but the prevalent thirst outside of him.

Concerning the inverted process, it is true that the poem presents an early "disclaimer" in which the regular process is tacitly affirmed: the first six lines of the opening stanza *do* identify the thirst with human sensibility, and only with the following nature-details does the inverted order take over. The word, "reflections," ambivalently suggests the merging of the human sensibility and the material world.

Then what is the big to-do about? For, apparently, the craftsmanship is not indulging an idle oxymoronic curiosity.

It seems that the explanation resides in the words, "human sensibility" and its intrinsic burden of thirst *and* fulfillment—because corollary to the idea proclaimed as the theme is this related idea that enhances it:

> The thirst for experience is not quenched by its
> contact with external agencies, for the human sensibility
> carries its own potentials for fulfillment and suitably
> "waters"
> these external forces by its own distinctive rain.

It's a fit corollary to enhance the theme, it seems.

So let the poem roam the granite country, it always finds its home in the human sensibility.

Format VIc. "Fisherman's Sonnet," Francis C. Macansantos

The four poems included in Format VI are not necessarily meant to justify here the melioration of free verse by adapting or reclaiming traditional elements into its liberated format. The four contemporary poems with their conventional admixtures are examples to show that the free-verse form is not violated or distorted but, on the contrary, as we have seen, it could even be allowed experimental development while keeping the neat and regulated influence of the traditional infusions. The following traditional features are mostly old and familiar elements appearing in

- "The Innocence of Solomon" and
- "Rain in Granite Country," both using rhyme and rhythm, and the latter poem cast in innovated structure;
- "Fisherman's Sonnet," using rhyme and rhythm and modified sonnet structure;
- "The Anteroom," using rhythm, a strong regularized metrical beat.

Fisherman's Sonnet

"And ye shall be fishers of men."

As the banca lolled on the water, we waited,
Father and I, for the tardy fish to bite.
The sea, rolling out to its rim and out of sight,
Counselled patience—indeed, exaggerated.
The sun hurt my skin, my eyes, but Father seemed elated.
Likely, he chose that day to set things right.
His patience with the fish, with me, held us tight
In a fishing-line bind that all but lacerated.

The rod he was wont to wield had sprung a line
Tipped with something I could only guess.
Whatever it was, I suspected a hook.
So why do I now cast lines into the benign
Ocean of his endless absence, lured with no less,
Perhaps, than love—the bait I once forsook.

As the title announces, "Fisherman's Sonnet" is a sonnet structure that we may describe as free-versely modified. No matter that, apart from the rhymed fourteen lines divided into octave and sestet, it does not follow the classic design (a rhyme scheme in mandated sequence; lines decasyllabic; octave presenting the argument, sestet the conclusion), yet it gracefully evokes the subjective feeling and concentrated involvement characteristic of the sonnet—with the possible difference that in this poem, paradoxically enough, these emotional components are vitalized by *restraint*. The consistent tone control keeps the persona's pathos and regret from breaking through the layer of harsh incidents and details that betray him as a son whose ill-disposition begot an equally ill-disposed son-father relationship.

Despite the acknowledged lack of amity, the impression of deep feeling hovers, the intense caring that somehow had not reached a mutual recognition or fulfillment—and in that situation lies the pathos, if not the tragic burden of the poem.

The persona's attitude of withdrawing or withholding and not reaching out is pervasive throughout the situations portrayed, showing him to be a habitually suspicious—or defensive—son; the father, though adversely pictured in the "rod he was wont to wield," initiates the move to bridge the gap ("to set things right").

The craftsmanship reaches its peak in the closing stanza, specifically in the last line, with the word *Perhaps*:

> So why do I now cast lines into the benign
> Ocean of your endless silence, lured with no less,
> *Perhaps*, than love—the bait I once forsook. (italics mine)

"Perhaps" is the acme; it caps the son's unconceding attitude; unconceding, that is, until the final phrase—and even then, the phrase qualifies the father's love by naming it "bait," a word which the son perfectly countermatches by qualifying his own faint conceding with the word, "lured."

The metaphorical structure is notably free of incongruities. In fact, there is a crucial thematic relevance in the choice of such details as "fishing-line," "fish," "rod," "ocean" and in the "fishing" structure, the meaningful linking of these sea-images to the persona's self-deprecated emotional crisis.

Apart from the Biblical epigraph—ironically relevant here—the words to clue into are "bait" and "lure," which underline the persona's suspicious and defensive attitude. Clearly, this fractious reaction refuses the Biblical "fishers of men," an injunction the persona perceives as a form of "hooking" a person, with love as the bait.

To be especially appreciated is the acuteness-with-words that worked the closing lines:

> So why do I now *cast lines* into the benign
> Ocean of your endless silence, lured with no less,
> Perhaps, than love—the bait I once forwsook. (italics mine)

The phrase, "cast lines," generates the exact though covert equivalent of an evoked phrase, "carve verses" (which is actually the persona's way of conceding his own reluctantly acknowledged *love/ lure/bait* for his father). Word for word, "cast lines" cannily breed both the literary translation and the *literal* transliteration of the evoked "carve verses." Very ingenious word usage, that. And warranting, if not warranted by, the sea-images.

The poem is distinguished by the consistent tone control, among the other effects sculpted by these internal poetry tools: inventive word usage, thematic tension, understatement, suggestiveness, alliteration, ambivalence.

Finally, why is the poem a topping example of Format VI, what justifies its modified adoption of the sonnet form? The controlled tone itself, as internal evidence, shows that this free-verse poem amply justifies the infusion of this particular traditional element; that is, despite the prickly material, the intense subjective involvement and lyricism inherent in the sonnet form not only gracefully offset the deeply basic harshness of the poetic substance and its pressing tension, but also, and more significantly, endow the poem with its ultimate pliancy and grace.

Format VId. "The Anteroom," Denise Levertov

Our fourth example of free verse admixed with traditional elements is written by a British-born writer, one of the freest of free-verse writers among the first rank of contemporary American poets. Characteristically with a good number of the poems of Denise Levertov, their mere appearance on the page confirms the stimulating zigzag of the lines as free verse worked veritably free indeed—although this is also saying that majority of her poetry lines are created in some regular stanzaic form or another.

In the following poem, the admixture of strongly regularized rhythm invests the format with the familiar attributes of orderliness and warm lyric appeal that are often missed in free-verse poems.

The Anteroom

Out of this anteroom whose light is broken
by slatted blinds and rustling portieres,
a tentative room too near the street,
pierced with street voices and the sound of horns,
uneasy halting place of traveling ghosts:

out of this season of uprooted hours,
where time, that should grow round as hanging fruit,
rushes like showers of dry and shrivelled leaves,
and no hour quickens into truth; where love,
confused, can never touch or penetrate
a growing dream, but hovers at its side:

that love, that dream, must travel
into wide landscapes where the heart has rest,
and quietly (as stones, pure on the still earth,
await a strange completion into dream,
by the slow rain, or by a man's desire)
await their transformation into life.

Particularly when read aloud, the poem, "Anteroom," immediately arouses an emotional reaction, and responsible for the quick stir of feeling is the rhythmic beat of the lines. The measured phrases are propelled by their dynamic cadences that ratify the reading of the words—for the well-defined pulsing tempo creates the connotative prods and pauses and accents, a slowing down here and a quickening there that present the articulation at its lyrical and meaningful best. An example:

> and no hour quickens into truth; where love,
> confused, can never touch or penetrate
> a growing dream, but hovers at its side.

This poem of three stanzas is a meditation on the human destiny to *await* any expected fulfillment, while feeling confined and cramped within the fore-span of anguish and uncertainty. The metaphorical anteroom, the "tentative room," is the antecedent period of befogging and befuddlement when the dream that is awaiting its time of fulfillment—or failure—appears only as a suspended alembic promising no definable shape or possibility of shape.

The anteroom of this poem is a kind of trap sprung by the human creature's own *sensibility*—which is his potent attribute as a higher organism, though it makes him, ironically, more vulnerable to stress or distress, or even to the wonted apprehensions about the outcome of any dream or scheme.

Artistic tension is produced by the substance and its articulation, the former steeped in uncertainty and tentativeness, the latter definite and firmly controlled by a strongly functional rhythm.

The poem dramatizes the situation as in a "tentative room" where the waiting is played out "too near the street," reminder that the experience is a normal part of the daily nitty-gritty and is no refined esoteric circumstance:

"pierced with street voices and the sound of horns"

Accordingly, the human sensibility lodges in the frustrating "anteroom waiting-span" and its concomitant angsts, and materializes these innuendoes and abstractions into the metaphoric images representing the unsettling physical and ruminated attributes of the anteroom:

- a tentative room too near the street
- uneasy halting place of traveling ghosts
- ... this season of uprooted hours

The second stanza is pitched on a high lyrical note that is sustained to the end of the poem. This stanza is a plaint picturesquely worded in withered-nature metaphors: time is "like showers of dry and shriveled leaves" for having been denied the "grow(ing) round as hanging fruit." And both time and love are perceived in this stanza as forces rendered powerless to ameliorate the as yet amorphous dream.

The final stanza's meditating voice considers the two conditions required for the dream to reach fulfillment. One, subsumed now by love, the dream needs the "wide landscapes" where it must have freedom from frazzling influences like anxiety and heartache and trepidation. It must reach its full reality in peace, "where the heart has rest."

Two, it achieves its "strange completion" in the way of the pure and natural forces like stones, and processed by the slow rain and—in the intriguing rather cyclic development of the poem—by the vitalizing generated from the *natural* unencumbered human need ("man's desire"). It is to be recalled that "man's desire" is, early on, the unspoken but pre-indicated motivation dredged up from the bootless lamentations of the first two stanzas—and we find it operative in the last stanza.

Instrumental in the craftsmanship is the strong rhythmic beat urging upon certain words and phrases the strategic impulsions and hesitations and emphatic accents that enhance the articulation, and make the reading, aloud or silent, an eloquent experience in itself. A clear example is indicated in the last four lines of the closing stanza which are replete with slowings and pauses and run-ons and induced accents caused by the energetic operation of the rhythmic measure:

> and quietly (as **stones, pure** on the **still earth,** [*pauses induced*]
> **await** a strange completion into dream, [line in *regular beat*]
> by the slow rain, or by a man's desire) [*slowed first phrase; quickened second phrase*]
> **await** their transformation into life. [line is *back to regular beat*]

Notable also is the synthetic merging of these last four lines of the poem.

Always a wholly integrated procedure: rhythm is imposed upon words and phrases; rhythm is created by the action of words and phrases—all in achieving the ultimate objective, which is the revelation of poetic meaning.

Touchstones from Contemporary Philippine Poets*

From *Gémino H. Abad:*

On the Law and its pronouncements:

Justice, they say, has scales over its eyes
where words bear holy weight of writ,
the same words shall hang the judge!
    Cry equity, cry compassion,
but these are words again,
and break where our victims lie.

On spoofing the technological era:

And young girls gape and faint
At his great wakeful Thing,
Well-hung, like a chandelier.

From *Rowena T. Torrevillas:*

On fitness and symmetry:

Two new legs (the fishtail split
As an egg's perfect circle
Broken by a hair) side by side
With a sorrow
Beyond all
Symmetry.

---

* Included in "*Pagsubay*: Resounding Contemporary Poetic Articulating"[4]

From *Alfred A. Yuson:*

On the "perks" afforded by contemplating a young loved child:

... His flight
of heart and lips is the first
chance and the finest sport,
a show of wisdom beyond all
hours vanished into daze.

From *Ophelia Dimalanta:*

On contending with quotidian rodent menace:

... to kill or not to,
Whether it's safer to let live.
Which is the greatest horror,
Death's fixity, a glassy stare,
Once and for all, and the ghost of it,
The reek, the sight of its absence there,
Or the scary hassle with the live
And vilely moving, a moving, scuttling
Scurrying shape along one's way or
Upon the margins of one's daily eyepath.

From *Marjorie Evasco:*

On being lost, and finding by certain guides, the way "out of the woods":

It was this burning tree of memory
Led him back to that first theft
When human eye beheld god's fire,

Singeing the imagination to waking.
He found his way out of the forest when
Seed, flower and trunk were forged in flame.

From *D. M. Reyes:*

On "insighting" eternity in the intimations of Space:

the beach tendered this view
always widening to hold
some things not really there.

More Touchstones from Contemporary Philippine Poets

From *Cesar R. Aquino, "Point of View,"* Checkmeta: The Cesar Ruiz Aquino Reader[5]

On a potent but unspoken communication with a stranger:

> but we are free,
> whatever wind we raise is for our minds
> and the thunder only

From *Ernesto S. Yee, "Saprid's Man Taming the Tikbalang,"* Covenants and Other Poems[6]

On giving shape and illumination to "spooks" and hobgoblins:

> Only when one meets his feared *Tikbalang*
> Eye to eye, will he cease to pull
> Hair, and the moon will be,
> Just.

Seven Exemplary Workshop Poems

With the exception of two titles, the seven poems following below were submitted by four Fellows of the 2003 National Writers Workshop; the two titles are by a poet from a previous year. The choices could have included other exemplary poems from previous Workshops, but as explained below, there is a reason, if perhaps rather specious (some would think!), for selecting from the 2003 Workshop.

For some years now I have believed in the paramount usefulness of a monograph that will present the distinction between free-verse poetry and the variety that is actually eloquent prose cut up into "verse-line" format. More and more of the latter is being written and presented as poetry.

About the 2003 Workshop, it was a certain unusually fine quality in some of the poems that confirmed for me the need to make such a definitive monograph available; a few of those submitted indicated a high order of conceptualizing which I also remarked in other poems in previous Workshops—that, and a second quality: the inventive insights and fresh perceptions, which are the marks of real/ potential talent at work.

Strangely enough, it was the confrontation with these qualities relating to the poetic *substance*, and not to the craftsmanship, that was directly responsible for the decision to write this monograph on poetry formats—or perhaps it is not so strange after all because, with certainty—and given the proper learner—the writing skill can be taught or caught; but teaching the writer who is without the intrinsic requirement of substance and ideas, to get him to perceive and conceive poetically is the epitome of the late Paul Engle's famous "trying to grow hair on a billiard ball."

So, my great thanks and accolade to these seven poems and their authors, and I look forward to the forthcoming workshop years that will continue the heart-warming trend.

She Who Jumped as a Tragedy

The physicist passing
was not surprised.

He calculated the force,
She was inertia,
regardless of the tattoo
on the left thigh,
near the pubic hair,
and the supple breast's
defiant nipple.

Nothing was wrong with
the orange building.
How much heartache she had,
the well-swept ground has matched it.

—Jonathan D. Davila

New Hampshire

This is a place of rock and ice.
Here the unforgettable of dead leaf and callow petal grows
like leaves.
And so I come to think of the both of you.

You, my beloved, the Fall, I understand them now:
Riddle of hues; wind's thinking growing colder
Rationalizing sky into granite; stillness that moves, the grin.
And, you, the Spring, you rush into my arms at last!
Now none is as shrewd as the blithe green; silent heart of
land
Finally grows quiet; flow that pauses, the wink.

Come to me, both of you, where you are safe
From my denuded affections and afflictions. I am wise now
As cold mud, I promise you.
So love me like beasts, like the wilderness.
Love me like the ground, like the unspeakable sun.

I am beautiful!

It is I,
Winter.

—George Ramos[7]

Iron Maiden

"It is also said that this sort of sarcophagus had the face of a maiden carved on its front door, probably with the aim of making this horrible container look more refined ... The inside of the sarcophagus was designed to pierce the different parts of the body, but miss the vital organs, so that the victim was kept alive, in an upright position."

~from www.torturamuseum.com~

My lady,

She does not

speak.

And yet,

so perfect is the shape

of every unformed

word,

It was as if

I get to

peer out

of her

lips

and wish

I had not

known.

—Ken Ishikawa

T. S. Eliot at Lloyd's

I had never really relished the smithing of words.
Actually, I had always wanted to be a banker,
A splendid sorcerer of the great INCs, invoking
The power of the number. But at university
Strange spells put such dreams to sleep, gently.
And the dreadful truths of poem, play and essay
Lent addictive ease to wakefulness. And then,
The first years: exultation so bleak, so bizarre
With the fierce beauty of being so close to
The Substance! I still dread to be a maker.

Then Vivien came to me, with all the hardiness
Of an agreeable realism. I, exalted, became heat
Of a sunless, humid day and its small agonies—
And its sweat. That is when I joined Lloyd's.
And reality flowed through me like a dream:
As fast as thoughts flee; as strange and lovely
As the random faces and spaces, persuading;
And as magical as a candlelit and disappointing
Night of Love with you, dear darling Viv—
Enchantress! All I wanted was a mild affair.

'Lord, forgive me for feasting on the fruit of
The tree of knowledge of good and evil.
Lord, forgive me for feeding a courage
To fight my rightful share of little deaths.
Lord, forgive me for feeling frightened
Of walking in darkness, eyes calmly shut.
Lord, forgive me for loving another more
Than You. Break my bow, O Jehovah, say I,
King Nimrod, for the heart of things
Is too hard to bear! Amen, my Lord, Amen.'

—George Ramos

Placelessness

No one lives here
but all you who left and are always leaving.
Memory is dust by the windowsill
that age gathers and grays
and thickens by a smoked window.
I turn inside my skin
the way walls turn inside theirs,
the slow crumble of stone, the unheard
shuffle of world when we close our eyes.
Sound of feet leaving.
You would not stay.
Memory, too, is distance
as soon as it leaves us. When
I walk, my feet leave each other behind.
I keep the windows closed and do not
look outside. All that is ahead is all that will remain.
The soil is this air, packed tight.
All that can move is moving,
and all that does not moves still.

—Vincent Esquejo Coscolluela

Mother

You caught me uncasing
Your blue eye shadow,
crushing it into powder,
coloring and caressing
my cushion-soft cheeks
with each round stroke
of my pointer. You had
known I would do this. You
had seen me—blue-booted toddler
of two—hover, and flit
through your beautifying
variety. From flesh-toned
foundation, to lavender
blush-on, then deep-black
mascara and rose-red

lipstick, you had only stared
in silence. You must have
hoped this phase would
fade, easy as the textures
and tints in your white and gold
vanity. Yet this love of beauty
grew, as dust stains
aged the drawers, finger-
prints marked the handles,
grey veins plagued
the mirror's silver face.
Your lips were pursed
as you pulled back the door,
the latch's lock signaling
the weight of reality.

—Niccolo Vitug

The End of a Frontier

Across the bridge and through the knolls
I stalked the river to a bend.

It was shallow there now and lahar
has covered most of what I remember;

but a long time ago, a Balete stood there
where once, one only had to wait

and squint at the moonlight to see
that the wind had bones and that the dark

has always been sentient—aware of its own
skulking mass. Now, only a stump remains

and I am old. Nothing fazes me anymore,
not even when what was left of the tree looked

like a severed waist from a distance.
Long ago too, they say there was a capre here,

who stalked beyond the area of the lamps
our elders lit to lore. No tracks of him remain,

No remains though the land hints of his skeleton.
I shuddered from the cold, walked home,

regretting how it was easy now to get there.
Then suddenly, I tripped on an upturned root

and saw how the ash scintillated its spread
diamonds in the dark and that wonder

still exists, hiding in the littlest of talismans.

—Ken Ishikawa

To Bind the Free: By Way of Summation

The six poetry formats demonstrated in this monograph have shown that a poem is primarily metaphor and not the versified expository stating or recounting of its meaning: Without the metaphoric structure there is no poetry.

The second poetic quality demonstrated by the formats is the enrichment of the poem's substance through the use of internal poetry devices and, even further, by the resonant corollary meanings evoked. We find these two qualities—metaphoric structure and conceptual enhancement—eminently important in the writing of free verse today.

Metaphoric Structure

More and more of the free verse being written are actually expository prose statements; it follows logically that: first, the metaphoric procedure, as demonstrated in the six formats, affirms the primary way of "binding" or keeping free verse within poetry borders.

Internal Poetry Instruments

The second way demonstrated here for controlling free verse articulation is the judicious use of the internal poetry tools, which enhance, if not actually authorize, the development of the poetic meaning through the resultant heightening of the poem's language and the vitalizing of its insights.

Third Way

There is a third way and it is contingent on the use of the two indicated procedures. Although this third way, like Maritain's "Third Way," is also "contingent and necessary,"[8] it is neither complicated nor abstruse. In this third procedure, some traditional features are part of the free-verse format, the precisely regulated features which were once discarded, like rhyme, meter, rhythm, and conventional stanza patterning, among others.

Proper Borders

It is obvious that the order generated by formal limits, such as these traditional components, keeps any loose or free elements within their proper borders; in the third procedure demonstrated here, free verse is indeed meaningfully controlled by the established limits of the traditional format.

These "proper borders" (of which a good clutch of the free verse being written tends to be unaware) have been defined, and defined spikily, by Robert Frost on various occasions, like his reference to these limits as the rules without which writing poetry is like his aphoristic "playing tennis without the net." His last poems seem to have discarded these borders, but the "mastered" net is there, artfully rendered invisible, an awesome evidence of craft mastery.

No Pure Free Verse

There is no such thing as *pure* free verse fashioning from poem to poem its own autarchic format. Following Jacques Maritain proclaiming that to posit the "*pure* contingent" is implying that "nothing exists," we may assert here that such a thing as *pure* free verse also demolishes, so that in its vaunted purity "nothing exists" of poetry, there is only prose.

Endnotes

1. The blunt critical observation was made by Ernesto S. Yee after a quiet appraisal of the two poems.

2. Edilberto Tiempo, Miguel Bernad, and Edith Tiempo, *Introduction to Literature* (Quezon City: R. P. Garcia Publishing Company Inc., 1977), 311-12.

3. Milton Ellis, Louise Pound, and George Weida Spohn, eds., *A College Book of American Literature* (New York, Chicago, et al.: American Book Company), 844.

4. An article by Edith L. Tiempo included in *Pagsubay: Graduate School Journal of the Eastern Visayas State University*, vols. 3 and 4 (2003-2004; 2004-2005). Edited by David Genotiva.

5. These are the last three lines of the poem, "Point of View," last published in *Checkmeta* (Davao City: Midtown Printing Co. Inc., Book Development and Publishing Division, 2003), 100.

6. These four lines comprise the last stanza of "Saprid's Man Taming the *Tikbalang*," from *Covenants and Other Poems* (Quezon City: Giraffe Books, 1999).

7. George Ramos was a fellow in the 1992 National Writers Workshop. He is still actively writing poetry, though, so far as is known, not submitting them for much-deserved publication.

8. The reference is to "The Third Way: By the Contingent and the Necessary" by Jacques Maritain, a selection from his *Approaches to God* (1955) and included in *Religion from Dostoevsky to Camus*, Introduction by Walter Kaufmann (New York and Evanston: Harper Torchbooks, Harper and Row), 380-82.

"The Third Way" is a very abstruse dissertation confuting the hypothesis of St. Thomas Aquinas-posited "*pure contingent*"; it is only very tangentially related to "the third way" of controlling free-verse articulating.

Bibliography

Abad, Gémino H. A *Makeshift Sun*. Quezon City: University of the Philippines Press, 2001.

Abad, Gémino H., and Alfred Yuson, eds. *One Hundred Love Poems*. Diliman, Quezon City: The University of the Philippines Press, 2004.

___________. *Father Poems*. Pasig City, Philippines: Anvil Publishing, Inc., 2004.

Aquino, Cesar. *Checkmeta: The Cesar Ruiz Aquino Reader*. Davao City: Midtown Printing Co. Inc., 2003.

Cavalli, Patrizia. "Far from kingdoms" and "Now that the time seems all mine." In *The Vintage Book of Contemporary World Poetry*, ed. J. D. McClatchy. New York: A Division of Random House, Inc., 1996.

Ellis, Milton, Louise Pound, George Weida Spohn, eds. *A College Book of American Literature*. New York: American Book Company, 1940.

Frost, Robert. *The Robert Frost Reader*. Library of Congress Cataloguing, Publication Data, ed. Edward Connery.

Jennings, Elizabeth. *Collected Poems, 1953-1985*. New York: Carcanet Press Ltd., 1987.

Levertov, Denise. *Denise Levertov: Collected Earlier Poems*. New York: New Directions Publishing Corporation, 4th printing, 1979.

Maritain, Jacques. *Approaches to God*. New York and Evanston: Harper and Row, Harper Torchbooks, 1955.

McClatchy, J. D. *The Vintage Book of Contemporary World Poetry*. New York: A Division of Random House, Inc., 1996.

Tiempo, Edith L. *Marginal Annotations and Other Poems*. Quezon City: Giraffe Books, 2001.

___________. "*Pagsubay*: Resounding Contemporary Poetic Articulating." In *Pagsubay: Graduate School Journal of the Eastern Visayas State University*, vols. 3 and 4, 2003-2004, 2004-2005. Edited by David Genotiva.

Tiempo, Edilberto, Miguel Bernad, Edith Tiempo, *Introduction to Literature*. Quezon City: R.P. Garcia Publishing, 1997; Manila: Rex Bookstore, 1989.

Torrevillas, Rowena T. *Mountain Sacraments*. Manila, Philippines: De La Salle University Press, 1991.

Yee, Ernesto S. *Covenants and Other Poems*. Quezon City: Giraffe Books, 1999.

___________. *About My Garden*. Quezon City: Giraffe Books, 2001.

Yuson, Alfred A. *Sea Serpent*, Quezon City: Monsoon Press, 1980.

The Author

Named National Artist for Literature in 1999, Edith L. Tiempo was born in Bayombong, Nueva Vizcaya, and spent her childhood years in Pasig and Manila. She later moved along with her family to Surigao, to which she would return after finishing her studies in Manila. She married writer Edilberto Tiempo in 1940 and they moved to Dumaguete City where Edilberto taught at Silliman University. She graduated magna cum laude from Silliman, and later earned an MA from the University of Iowa and a PhD from the University of Denver. In 1962 the Tiempos organized the National Summer Writers Workshop at Silliman, the first of its kind in the Philippines. She has taught at Western Michigan University and Wartburg College in the US, and at the Chinese University of Hong Kong and Hong Kong Baptist College. Her poetry has won the Palanca Memorial Award and her novel, *His Native Coast*, was awarded first prize by the Cultural Center of the Philippines. In 1988, she and Edilberto were awarded the Gawad Pambansang Alagad ni Balagtas by the Unyon ng mga Manunulat sa Pilipinas (UMPIL). "Mom Edith" has published four collections of poetry, one collection of short stories, four novels, and three textbooks.

